Creating With The Law of Attraction

10 Principles that will Change Your Life

Edward J. Langan

iUniverse, Inc.
New York Bloomington

Creating With The Law of Attraction

iUniverse books may be ordered through booksellers or by contacting:

iUniverse
1663 Liberty Drive
Bloomington, IN 47403
www.iuniverse.com
1-800-Authors (1-800-288-4677)

ISBN: 978-0-595-52216-3 (sc)
ISBN: 978-0-595-62276-4 (ebook)

Printed in the United States of America

iUniverse rev. date: 12/29/2008

Dream your life. Live your dream.
Be your bean.™

www.BeYourBean.com

Dedicated, in loving memory, to:
John Langan, Kenny Langan, Joey Melanson, and Joseph Melanson.

Acknowledgments

It's been said the two most powerful words are thank you. As I study the law of attraction, I've learned that when you are grateful and appreciating you are your highest self and in harmony with your inner being. The following words do not begin to accurately describe my thanks, gratitude and appreciation to and for the following people.

My parents, John and Louise Langan. You inspired my wonder of life, quest for knowledge, my joy of teaching and sharing with others. Our venture years ago set me on this path. Thank you.

Thank you to Jason Straw, Sara Moore, and everyone at iUniverse. Marj and I love this book and appreciate all your efforts.

The photo on the back cover is from our dear friends Lynda Read and Susan Bouchard of Options Photography. Thank you, we love the fun we have with you.

Thank you Marlisa Clapp, Pam Marcella, and Samantha Jones of MCD Studios for our amazing website. www.BeYourBean.com. And thank you Marlisa Clapp for the beautiful art direction of the cover.

Ann Donohue, thank you for your insights and attention to details. You are brilliant. Thank you Amanda Hamm, Debbie Andrade, Jean Schwier, Greg De Stephano, and Jim Garvey for your thoughts and insights, they are appreciated.

Thank you Hannah Goodman for your kindness, ideas, and efforts in editing this book, you helped me focus the book and make it much better. www.hannahrgoodman.com

The book you are holding in your hand would not be, if not for the help of my wife Marjorie. Thank you for your tireless effort, insights, ideas, love, help and support. I am honored and humbled by your love and belief in me.

Table of Contents

Introduction

This book is inspired by the teachings of Abraham-Hicks. It's based on everything that I've learned so far, filtered through my beliefs and my life experiences. My journey began when I started asking myself questions about my life and the way I was living it. The journey has led me to share what I have learned, what has worked for me, and what has helped me answer those questions. I know a lot of you seek answers to those same questions I had (and still have), and now, all that asking has led you to this book.

Simply put, there's a lot of information here. Together, you and I are going to cover a lot of ground. I'll be here to guide you the whole way. But first I'd like to tell you a little about me, and my journey.

My Journey

Two events in my life caused me to question how I was living. My youngest brother and my younger cousin both died suddenly. I had already been a seeker all of my life with a great thirst for knowledge. Their passing really intensified my focus and desire for answers. Although a lot of questions about God and the universe came up within me, the strongest questions that presented themselves to me were: *What is left here for me? What am I doing with my life? What is important to me? What do I want to accomplish?*

From these questions came a quest for knowledge and enlightenment. I wanted to know everything. And I studied everything:

- Silva Mind Control®
- Super Learning Music
- Meditation Practices
- The Avatar Material
- A Course In Miracles
- The Science Of Deliberate Creating And The Art Of Allowing from Abraham-Hicks
- Native American Religion
- Self-Hypnosis and The Turning Point Seminar
- Near Death Experiences

Armed with everything I studied, I felt compelled to write this book. I feel that it answers the questions I have been asking for years. Questions that you probably are asking, too. Here's a preview of what follows.

Overview

As a musician, music has always been the voice of the universe to me, a way of expressing the inexpressible. I use music as a metaphor throughout this book. However, you don't have to be a musician to understand what I'm saying.

You can't play a musical scale until you know what notes to play, and you can't play a melody til you know what scale to use. Chapters one through seven will give you the notes. Chapters eight through eighteen show you how to play the melody. Each of the first chapters builds on to the next one to make a solid bass line, a strong foundation for understanding.

You are going to learn about creating with the law of attraction. You'll learn the 10 principles that will change your life. You might look at your life and want to improve it, find a new focus, a new career, whatever matters to you. You get to decide why you are using these principles. You can use them to create whatever you want.

I'll explain what our emotions really are and why we have them, as well as how to use them rather than be controlled by them. You'll learn what the law of attraction is and how to apply it to your life. You will see how quantum physics and spirituality can blend together. You will see who and what you really are. I will illustrate the power of thoughts and show you how what you believe creates what happens in your life. You will discover which of your beliefs are working for you and which ones are not. You will learn how to change those beliefs that don't work and create new ones.

I will reintroduce you to your imagination, show you how powerful it is, and teach you how to use it to your advantage. We're going to talk about the importance of asking. What desire is and what it can do for you. We're going to talk about the Zen principal of being in the moment. You will learn why "now" is the most important moment there is.

I'll show you the emotional scale and teach you how to move up the scale towards feeling better. I'll talk about the turbulence and drama in your life and what you can do about it. You'll understand what is "good" and "bad" and who gets to decide. You will learn the awesome power of forgiveness and why it is so important to you and your life. There will be exercises mixed in along the way, as well as a whole chapter of exercises all of which are designed to help you change your life.

I believe in the material in this book. I know it works. In chapter six, you are going to learn the importance of what you believe. I know that if you do the exercises and study the material in this book, your life will change. I'm absolutely sure of that. The process, thoughts, and ideas that I outline in this book will work, but it really comes down to the old joke, "How do you get to Carnegie Hall? Practice, practice, practice." You have to practice these methods that I'm going to give you. If you do, your life will change, forever.

The Next Step

Now you know a little bit about why I wrote this book. Life is a journey, an adventure. Where you go next is entirely up to you. I hope this information makes a huge difference in your life. The next step is to read this book. The step after that is to practice the exercises. What I said earlier bears repeating. The first seven chapters are individual notes. Each one builds upon the next, fitting them together like a melody. After the first seven chapters, you'll have a solid foundation and an understanding of the basics. You may have to accept some things on faith until you fully understand them in the later chapters of the book. As you read the first seven chapters, try to keep an open mind and withhold your judgment. The payoff will be well worth it. The chapters need to be read in order so that you understand the concepts as they build on each other. After you've read the book once and done some of the exercises, read the parts of the book and do the exercises that resonate with you. Do them again and again. My goal for you is that your book becomes worn, dog-eared, and well used. Your journey starts with the first step. The next step is, turn the page...

1

The Principles

Your mind thinks in pictures not in words. When you close your eyes and imagine or visualize, you don't see words, you see pictures. When you're asleep and dreaming, your mind's eye rarely sees words floating by. Instead, you see objects, people, places, and things. You see scenes.

When we communicate, the words we use generate images. Words can mean different things to different people, and so can the images generated by these words. For example, if I tell you about a fishing trip I took to a New Hampshire lake, I will picture the largemouth bass I caught, the lake I was fishing in, and all the stumps and lily pads in that lake. You might picture something different, like a deep, clear, cold lake, full of trout.

The word "God" invokes strong meaning and generates different pictures in each of us. My image of God used to be the traditional father figure archetype; long flowing robes, a long white beard, lightning bolts at the ready, passing judgment on us mere mortals. Some people have no image of God because they don't believe, and the word conjures no images at all. Still others may picture God in a less traditional manner. When they hear the word "God", they may feel the warmth of the sun, or envision a quiet walk in the forest. The possibilities are endless.

Because the word "God" can conjure up so many meanings, both good and bad, I will refer to "God" as "universe". What I mean by "universe" is God-force, life-force, source, collective consciousness, infinite intelligence, inner being, love, or any energy that is considered to be good.

I want you to hear the messages in this book and not get hung up on the meaning of any words. The important thing is to understand the underlying principles I discuss and then understand how to use them in your life.

My goal is to explain these principles to you in a way that is easy to understand. Then, you will be able to apply them to your life. I'm going to give you a brief explanation of each of the principles, and in the chapters ahead, I will go into greater detail.

The principles:

1. How you feel is important.

Your emotions help you navigate through life. They tell you how you are doing and whether or not you're moving towards or away from what you want. Did you ever notice that you if you wake up in the morning feeling bad, you carry that feeling with you all day? This feeling means more than just you feeling bad. It means that you're moving away from what you want. In chapter two, you will learn what your feelings really are, and what they are telling you.

2. The law of attraction controls everything.

The definition of the law of attraction is this: Things that are similar or the same attract each other. Did you ever have a day where everything just seemed to go perfectly? You felt good and good things kept happening all day long. Did you ever have one of *those* days where everything just seemed to go wrong? It was like there was a little black cloud over your head. In both cases, the law of attraction was working with you, creating your day. I'm going to explain to you how to use the law of attraction in your life to create the things you want. You will learn how to make the law of attraction work for you in chapter three.

3. The universe always says yes and does not give up on you.

There is no such thing as "no" in this universe. The universe will keep trying over and over to give you what you want. Did your parents give up on you when they were teaching you how to walk? They never said, "I helped you forty times, and each time you've fallen down, so I'm not going to help you any more." The universe never gives up on you either. I'm going to show you how the universe helps you to manifest the things that you want in your life. In chapters three and seven you will gain full understanding of this principle.

4. You create your own reality.

Whether you realize it or not, you are here to create your life. Whatever you want.

You don't need to prove anything to anyone. You don't need anyone's permission. In chapter four, we will talk about quantum physics and the universe, and how it can help you to create your own reality.

5. You create your own reality, even if you don't know you're doing it.

People who have schizophrenia or multiple personality disorder can have a completely different physiology for every one of their personalities. For example, one personality might need to wear glasses, another personality may be diabetic, and still another personality may have a completely different menstrual cycle.. Once you understand that you create your own reality, I will teach you how to create it on purpose, which we will talk about in chapter four.

6. There is plenty for everyone.

The universe is based on abundance. There is more than enough for everyone, and you can allow yourself to have it. Just look around. There are examples of the abundance of the universe everywhere.

Everything is teeming with abundance from the smallest quantum particles to the largest mountains. Look at the leaves on the trees, and the stars in the sky. The universe shows you its abundance. If you look for it, you will find it. You will learn about the abundance of the universe in chapter four.

7. Thought is everything, and everything is thought.

Everything started from thought. Everything you can see, hear, and feel was at one time a thought. Thoughts about the wheel were inspired by the need to move things. Someone saw a rock or a log roll down a hill and was inspired with more thought. Eventually they came up with the wheel and the axle. More thought and wagons and carts evolved. If you look around today, you will see wheels everywhere. Everything starts from thought. I will explain this fully in chapter five.

8. The life you are now living is what you believe.

The sum total of your life right now was created by everything that you believe up to this point. If you believe you can, you can, and you're right. If you believe you can't, you can't and you're *still* right. The beliefs you have create the foundation of your life. We will explore this fully in chapter six and learn how to change and create new beliefs that can help you create the life you want.

9. You are worthy.

Right now, exactly as you are, you're completely worthy. Worthy of everything you want. Think about nature and all of its beauty and complexity. A flower only lasts a few days, a sunset a few minutes; while you last a lifetime. You are smarter than the best computers on earth. They can't do what your brain can do. You are a complex, unique individual who can think, create, and wonder. As artist M.C. Escher said, "He who wonders discovers that this in itself is wonder." You can imagine, think, and ponder. We are the only creatures who can do this. You can write, draw, and make music. You can love, feel, inspire, and learn. You can touch and move others with your thoughts, your words and what you create. You are a miracle. You are an amazing, magnificent being right now, exactly as you are. You are worthy. Chapter fourteen will help you improve your self-esteem.

10. Life is meant to be fun.

I hope that this is self-explanatory. Life is meant to be fun. Life is meant to be joyful. Life is meant to be enjoyed. Look at children, how ready they are to laugh and play. Almost anything can bring them joy and fun: an empty box, a block, a stuffed animal, a stick, a flashlight, or a ball. No child is born a cynic or a pessimist. They learned that from adults. Just as they learned to stop being a kid, and get serious about life. Seriousness is a trait of the ego, not of your inner being. Fun, joy, laughter, eagerness, and enthusiasm are all traits of your inner being, which were natural in you when you were a child and are still within you now. In chapters eight and ten you will reconnect with the idea that life is meant to be fun.

The chapters that follow in the book will weave these principles together, and you'll see that these 10 principles are the keys to changing your life.

2

Emotions

It wasn't until after I felt the joy of an "aha" moment that I knew which subject should be first in this book. This chapter on emotions is the most important. **If you don't read anything else in this book, read this chapter. The information I'm about to give can change your life, if you follow and use it.**

"Nothing is more important than that I *feel* good!"
-- Abraham-Hicks.

What are emotions? Why do we have them? If we can feel them, it's obvious that they are trying to tell us something. What do they do? And what are they trying to tell us? Our emotions are communication from our higher self to our conscious self. Our emotions are how we navigate through our life. Yes, both men and women have this ability, although women usually find it easier to identify what they are feeling. Our emotions are telling us how we are doing in relationship to what we want. When we decide that there is something that we would like, the universe starts forming the energy around it, and we can "feel" it. We feel good when what we are thinking and/or doing is in harmony with what we would like. We feel bad when what we are thinking and/or doing is not in harmony with what we would like. This is how we use our emotions to navigate.

Our emotions are very important. However, society has taught us to guide ourselves from the outside. What I said in the previous paragraph bears repeating: Our emotions are communication from our higher self to our conscious self. Our emotions are how we navigate. Our emotions are the way the universe communicates with us.

Our emotions are telling us how we are doing in relation to what we want. When we feel good, what we want is coming to us. When we don't, we're impeding what we want from getting to us. It's almost like we're creating friction within our own system.

If you drove your car without putting oil in your engine, it would create lots of friction. If you could feel the friction, the heat, and the discomfort of your engine, you would stop immediately. This is how we use our emotions to navigate. If we feel discomfort inside ourselves, we stop and try to make it better. We put "oil" in the "engine" so we can "drive" smoothly again.

Some of us use therapy or a long walk to soothe ourselves. When we feel internal friction, we stop and try to get what we need or want to make ourselves feel better. However, this only works if we are paying attention to how we are feeling. A lot of us have been trained to ignore our feelings so we don't know what we want, and, therefore, we remain unhappy and dissatisfied with our lives. Knowing what you feel helps you to know more about what you want. When you know what you want, you can "put it out to the universe" and the universe will communicate back to you by giving you what you want.

A new home

A women at one of my workshops asked me, "How do I get a new house?" Do you remember the first part of Principle three: **The universe always says yes?** I explained to her, that as you are thinking about the new house, the universe starts an energy vortex around the thought of you living in your new house, and as I said earlier, you can literally feel it.

I said to her, "You want to think thoughts about your new home that feel good to you. Can you think of any thoughts about the new house that feel good to you?" "OK, she said, "it will be bigger so there will be more room for all of us and we will each have our own space. I will have my dream kitchen and we will all hang out there together when friends and family come over and visit. It will have a nice living room with a cozy fireplace for the winter. It will have a master bedroom suite with a spa tub like I've always wanted. I can see my new furniture in the great room and the whole family being there for the holidays." Her eyes were alive with excitement. "How does that feel to you?" I asked. "It feels good," she said. "The energy vortex has started around you getting a new house. Those thoughts feel good so they are in harmony with what you want, and it's flowing to you."

"But what if we can't sell our house? It's really small and it's been on the market for awhile. The economy is bad and houses are not selling. This could lead us to financial ruin." The spark was gone from her eyes. I asked her, "How do those thoughts make you feel?" "Really bad," she replied. "What you are doing with those thoughts is creating friction,. Your feelings are telling you that the thoughts that you are thinking are not in harmony with what you said you wanted. If you keep thinking those thoughts, your new home, which was on its way, is no longer easily flowing to you."

So let me break this down in the simplest terms I possibly can: You decide you would like something. The universe agrees and begins to form energy around it. As you think about it, your feelings are telling you that when you feel good, what you want is flowing to you. When you feel bad, what you want is not flowing to you. That's how you navigate your life with your feelings.

Vacation vs. work

Let's navigate together through another example. What does it feel like when you wake up on the first day of your vacation? You're feeling eager and excited. You're happy. You're full of anticipation about where you're going. You practically jump out of bed. You can't wait to get your day started. If someone asks you how you are feeling, you would say you are in a good mood. Compare that to the morning when you get up to do something you don't want to do. Like going to a job that you don't like. The alarm goes off, you feel sluggish and don't want to get out of bed. You hit the snooze at least once, maybe more. You're tired, listless, or maybe even angry. You're certainly not eager and full of energy. Instead, you're slow and dragging. You feel anxious or bad. You're probably cranky with others around you. If someone asks you, you would probably say you're in a bad mood.

Let's look at the vacation example. You're eager, excited, you feel good. Your energy is flowing. Your emotions are telling you that you are in harmony with your desire. Now let's look at the example of working at a job that you don't like. You don't feel good, you're anxious and in a bad mood. Your emotions are telling you that what you are thinking is not in harmony with what you want. That's right, what you are thinking-your thoughts. Nothing else. What you are thinking brings forth an emotional response. Your emotions come from the thoughts that you think. They are the response to the thoughts that you are thinking. Always. What you are feeling is telling you if the thoughts you are thinking are in harmony with your desire or not. Chapter five is on thoughts. Remember what I said about reading this chapter? I recommend you read that chapter, too.

Two emotions

The thoughts that you are thinking only bring up variations of two emotions, feeling good or feeling bad. *A Course in Miracles* says there are only two emotions, love and fear. Abraham-Hicks says there are only two emotions– one feels good and one feels bad. Starting to see a trend here? We have given all kinds of names and all kinds of labels to all of our emotions. But if you think about it, they all fall into one category or the other. We have a long list of emotions that feel good: joy, happiness, enthusiasm, love, hope, optimism, etc. Conversely, we have a long list of emotions that feel bad: anger, blame, worry, hate, guilt, depression, fear, etc. Regardless of the label that you would give the emotion, it's easy to see that an emotion either feels good or feels bad. In essence, there really are only two emotions, and the labels that we give them are describing the intensity of the emotion rather than a different emotion.

Now some emotions feel really bad and others don't feel so bad. Some emotions feel really good, and others feel kind of good. The intensity of the emotion is an important part of the communication. If something happens that makes you very angry, what is being communicated to you is: this subject is very important to me. Because I'm feeling bad, what I am thinking and/or doing is creating friction within me and not letting my energy flow. This bad feeling is letting you know how much desire you have and how important this subject is to you. Anger and fear mean you have really strong desire, but the thoughts that you are thinking are really opposite of what you want. So you're not letting your energy flow.

What happens when something feels really good? The communication to you is: I am feeling really good, and so this subject is very important to me. I feel good. I'm not creating any friction within me, and I'm letting my energy flow fully, so my desire right now is easily coming to me. Finally, I am, right now, in perfect tune with my higher self and my conscious self. The strong feeling of joy and passion all mean that you're in harmony with your strong desire and that you're letting your energy flow.

For example, I remember being in art class. We were drawing the figure. One of the girls in the class was having a really hard time. She threw down her pencil, and complained a bit under her breath and walked out of the room. We all knew she was upset, and we all knew that she was a having a hard time with the drawing. A little later, she calmed down and came back in. We were having a group discussion and talking about our drawings and what we had done during that session. I said to her, "It's not a bad thing that you got as frustrated and upset as you did. What that means is that you really care about this. You really want to be able to draw well, and you really want to be able to draw the figure." She looked at me kind of perplexed, because she didn't understand what I meant. "How is my frustration at not being able to do this a good thing?" she asked me. "You saw me trying to do it, and you know I couldn't do it, and it just made me very upset. How is that good?" I explained to her that she has a really strong desire to be able to draw well and that if she didn't, she wouldn't care if she were unable to draw well. She wouldn't get upset, and she wouldn't get frustrated because she just wouldn't care and it wouldn't matter.

You only have strong energy flowing and strong desire about things that matter to you. If you don't care, it doesn't matter, and you don't get upset. Your feelings are telling you, this is important to me, but the thoughts that I'm thinking are not allowing it to come to me. As she was trying to draw, she was thinking, *this is a hard pose. I'm having trouble doing this. I'm not getting this right. I don't know if I can draw.* Those self-doubting thoughts are not consistent with what she wanted to do, which is to be able to draw the figure. When she was thinking things like that and trying to draw the figure at the same time, she could feel the conflict, and she got upset. She couldn't draw the figure, and the anger and frustration she was feeling was her navigation letting her know what she was doing. The thoughts that she was thinking right then were not allowing what she wanted to come to her. That's how your emotions work. That's what they are there for.

The emotional scale

The following is an emotional scale:

10. Love
9. Joy
8. Appreciation
7. Passion
6. Enthusiasm
5. Happiness
4. Belief
3. Trust
2. Optimism
1. Hope

0. Contentment
-1. Boredom
-2. Pessimism
-3. Frustration
-4. Worry
-5. Blame
-6. Discouragement
-7. Anger
-8. Revenge
-9. Hate
-10. Guilt
-11. Grief
-12. Depression

When we look at this scale, we can see that from 1 to 10 feels good. At times, contentment probably feels good, too. From -1 to -12, we can see that this side doesn't feel good. One to 10 and beyond is the "love" side. Zero to -12 is the "fear" side. From this, you can see, although there are many labels, that there are only two emotions, love and fear. The higher up on the scale, the more we are allowing our energy to flow and the better we feel. The lower down on the scale, the worse we feel because we are not allowing our energy to flow. Our energy flowing is how we attract and receive what we want. This concept will be explained throughout the rest of the book. If we think of this as a musical scale, then we want to keep moving up to the higher notes. We want to keep moving a few notes at a time and not trying to make big jumps. 1 to 10 is like a major scale, or happy music. Zero to -7 is like a minor scale, or sad music. -5 to -12 is like a diminished scale, or very sad music.

The main idea is to move up this scale. Although the scale illustrated above stops at 10, in reality, it doesn't. There is no limit to how good you can feel. You can just go higher and higher. As you recall in the introduction, I said that the chapters build on each other and fit together like a jigsaw puzzle. You will learn how to move up the emotional scale in chapter ten, *Giant Steps*.

How our emotions feel

Now let's review some of our emotions and what they feel like, especially for those of us who have forgotten or are not in touch with our feelings. Sorry guys, that's usually us. Let's start with the easy ones, like anger. What does it feel like when you are really angry? Well, let's look at some of the common expressions that are used to describe it and see if that gives us any insight: *I'm so angry I could explode. I felt like I was going to blow my top. That made me so mad, I could spit nails. If looks could kill...* All of those expressions describe feeling bottled up, feeling confined, feeling restricted, and feeling blocked. You're pulling more energy then you're allowing to flow. That strong feeling of pressure and suffocation is your indicator that you're not letting your energy flow. So, anger feels like a clog in a hose or like a blockage. That's why when people feel really angry, they tend to snap, explode, and lash out. They yell and scream and carry on to try to relieve the pressure, push the blockage out to let the energy flow again.

Now let's look at joy and what that feels like. Joy has the opposite feeling of anger. You feel happy, you feel eager, you feel energized, and you feel alive. When you're feeling this way, you usually can't sit still. Do you remember the end of the movie *Saturday Night Fever* with John Travolta? He was feeling so good that he wanted to strut down the street. That's a classic example of feeling good and what that looks like. We've all seen people who were very happy. They usually spread their arms out and up. They close their eyes, tip their head back, and smile. They appear to be basking in how good they feel. Some people, when they feel really good, start to dance, like Cuba Gooding Jr.'s character in *Jerry Maguire.* When you're feeling like this, you are fully connected with your higher self. You are in harmony with who you really are and your desires. You are wide open and letting the energy of the universe flow. The feeling is electric. It's exciting. It's enthusiasm, and we all feel the energy flowing, and that's why enthusiasm is contagious.

It's hard to describe feelings with words. There are not enough words to accurately describe all the feelings you feel. It's like trying to describe a color to somebody. You really can't describe the color so you say, "It's like this thing–" and you name an object that is the color you are trying describe or you say, "It kind of looks a little bit like this, except maybe a little bit lighter." Trying to describe feelings is trying to express the inexpressible. We struggle to find the right words, and, not being able to find them, we use metaphors and analogies. Because the best art and music create an emotional response within us, it seems that much of art and music are an attempt to describe feelings. Let's try to describe a couple more. Ladies, I can hear you. A guy talking about feelings! I know, amazing, isn't it?

What does it feel like to be in love? It feels good, it feels joyful, and it feels happy. You can feel light, almost like you're floating. You don't seem to mind the things that go wrong around you. You say things like: That's all right. I'm feeling too good to be bothered by that. I am not going to let that bring me down. You have all the feelings that we described in joy. You're fun to be around. You light up even more when you see your lover or talk to him or her on the phone. You feel like Leonardo DiCaprio and Kate Winslet from the movie *Titanic* in the scene where they're on the bow of the ship, and Leonardo proclaims, "I feel like the king of the world." Then he stands up on the bow, spreads his arms out, tips his head back, and closes his eyes.

Let's try another one. What do gratitude and appreciation feel like? Well, like being in love, they put a smile on your face. You feel open, and you may feel a warm feeling in the center of your chest. You feel expanded, and you feel full. You feel grateful. You might think to yourself, wasn't that a really nice thing they did? Gratitude is a hard one to describe. When you feel gratitude, you're at your best. That's when you're letting all your energy flow.

Have you ever run into a grocery store to buy one item? You're in a hurry, you rush into the store, find the item, and head for the checkout. You get to the express lane, and there's a woman just starting to check out and a man in front of you with a full cart of 15 items to check out. You get in line and nervously look at your watch. The woman is just about finished, and the man in front of you turns and says, "You only have one item. You can go ahead of me." Right there, in that instance, a wave of gratitude flows over you, from head to toe. You can't thank him enough. You really appreciate it. What a nice person he is to do that for you. And the amazing thing is, you didn't even ask.

All of the good feelings are open, expanding, and flowing. You feel empowered. You're letting all the good things you want flow to you when you feel good. All of the bad feelings, whatever names you want to call them, feel confining, constricting, and suffocating. They make you feel like you have no power. They create friction within you, and let you know that what you want is being hindered by what you're thinking. But the good news is, you can always change the way you feel by changing what you think. **Your feelings come in response to your thoughts, and you always have control of what you're thinking.** Once you feel better, you have your power back.

What happens to people when they're not in touch with their feelings? That depends on how much they are out of touch. For someone who is out of touch with her feelings, life can be a roller-coaster ride because she only notices really strong feelings. Since she doesn't know that her feelings are communication from her higher self and what she feels is in response to what she thinks and the strength of her desire, she finds it very disconcerting and confusing. The confusion and discomfort causes her to try to hide and ignore her feelings even more, which only starts a vicious cycle and makes the roller- coaster ride even worse. People who are so far out of touch with their feelings that they are numb can become dangerous. They don't feel good feelings, and they also don't feel bad feelings like: guilt, remorse, regret, or fear. So there's a potential for them to do harmful things. If you think about it, your conscience is a feeling. It's sort of a poke at you that says, "Maybe I shouldn't do this. This probably is not the best idea I've had." Your conscience communicates with you as a feeling.

So, to reiterate, your feelings are communication from your higher self to you. The strength of the feeling that you feel is telling you how important this thing is to you and if you are attracting the thing or hindering it.

Feelings can also overwhelm people. When you don't know what feelings are or why you're having them, this can be very disconcerting. You could end up feeling like a ping-pong ball. You bounce around all over the place, feeling all kinds of things. Some good, some bad, and some you're not even sure of. This bouncing around can lead to feeling overwhelmed, which can lead to addictions.

Addictions can be connected to feelings in two ways. First, people get so overwhelmed by their feelings that they become anxious and afraid of them. They try to stuff them back down with food, alcohol, drugs, etc. Second, deep down inside, we all know that it's natural to feel good. We want so much to feel good that we drug ourselves in some way or another to feel good. While we are high or intoxicated, we feel better because we've stopped thinking about what was bothering us. The problem is, we didn't find our way to feeling better by choosing our thoughts and paying attention to how they feel, instead, we found our way to the good feelings by getting high. So the only way we can get back to the state of feeling some relief is by continuing to get high. However, feelings don't go away if they are ignored or stifled. They tend to get stronger. It gets harder and harder to ignore them. In response, we use more of our drug of choice, and then the addiction gets stronger. That's when it becomes a problem.

What society teaches

Society teaches us to ignore our feelings, which really means ignore our navigation. We're taught to look outside of ourselves for answers. Have you heard the expression *if Mama ain't happy, nobody's happy?* We learn at an early age that if certain people are upset, it's better to ignore how we feel and either get out of their way, or do something to make them feel better. This is especially true for little children, who rely on other people for everything. We are taught at an early age what the appropriate behavior is for certain situations. We learn how to play roles. We learn how to wear masks and hide behind them. When you go to church, you are taught the appropriate behavior, and the way to act, regardless of how you feel. When you go to Grandma's house, you sit quietly in your chair and say please and thank you. There is no running around at Grandma's house, and we do not touch any of Grandma's things. We are taught to ignore our feelings, so instead of looking to navigate with our feeling radar, we start to look outside of ourselves for answers and for things that will make us happy.

The media is aware that people are looking outside of themselves to make them feel better, and to make them feel whole. Lynne Twist, highlights this idea in her book *Soul of Money Transforming Your Relationship with Money and Life*: "We start to believe the profit driven commercial and cultural messages that suggest money can buy happiness, and we begin to look outside of ourselves to be fulfilled."[1]

But the heaven you seek is **always** within. Nothing outside of us can guide us as well as we can guide ourselves.

Let's take a look at a few examples of how society teaches us to ignore our feelings and to lose track of how we navigate. People who are in the military are trained to ignore the feeling of fear and to rely on their training. For people who are going to be put in harm's way, this is a very effective way to train them. However, it also teaches them to ignore their navigation. Veterans returning from war sometimes suffer from post-traumatic stress disorder. They see horrific things, and they are not in a place where they can acknowledge what they're feeling. So they ignore and/or suppress what they're feeling while they're in combat situations. They run into trouble when they get home when feelings that they've suppressed start bubbling up again.

Society also teaches us which feelings are acceptable to show in public and which feelings are not. As I said earlier, by following this social norm, we begin to ignore what we're feeling and start to play roles. We start putting on masks to hide behind. I remember when I was a young boy, I was playing Little League baseball. I remember getting hit pretty hard in the arm with the baseball. I wasn't seriously hurt, but it was quite painful. I wanted to cry, but I remember being encouraged by the coach and by the rest of my teammates to "tough it out, walk it off, suck it up, and shake it off". "You are all right," they all told me. "Come on, let's go." What was

1 Twist, Lynn, *Soul of Money Transforming Your Relationship with Money and Life* W.W.Norton & Co. Inc. 2003

Tom Hanks' line from the movie, *A League of Their Own*? "There's no crying in baseball." So, with things like that, little by little, we start to lose track of our internal navigation.

I remember another time when I struck out and was very upset. In my opinion, I didn't help my team much at all. I wouldn't say it caused us to lose the game, but I didn't help us win it either. I was very upset, and again, I wanted to cry and have a little fit. But I didn't, because "I'm a man." I was just a little kid and knew that men didn't cry. So I didn't. I sucked it all in, slammed the bat to the ground, kind of lashed out in anger, and again moved away from my navigation and my internal radar.

Not saying what we mean

Another way we lose touch with our feelings is by not saying what we mean. A very small amount of our communication comes from what we actually say. How we feel is the biggest part of our communication with others. Children are very good at reading how others feel because they are still using their feelings to navigate with. They still trust their feelings.

For example, a man and woman are not getting along well. The woman is upset with the man because of something he did. They are in the living room in the middle of a disagreement. Their young son, hearing the commotion, leaves his bedroom upstairs and comes down to the living room to see what's going on. In order to protect the child, when he walks into the room, they pretend nothing is going on. The child, who is about five or six-years-old, is still very much in touch with how he navigates and his internal radar and can easily *feel* that both parents are upset.

There may be some visual clues, but adults do the best they can to hide the truth, which they believe is for the child's own good. What they don't realize is the child can tell, because he can feel it. He can easily feel that his mother is very upset because she doesn't hide her feelings as well as his father can. So the child asks, "Mommy, what's the matter?" And the mother replies, "Nothing honey." The child thinks, hum that's strange; I can feel that she's very upset. Why is she telling me she's not upset? The child asks again, “Mommy is everything okay? You don't seem like you're so happy to me?” And once again, the mother now visibly upset, tells the child in a curt manner, “ No, Mommy is fine.”

The child now turns and says, “Daddy, why are you mad?” By now the father is starting to get upset and says to the child, “Why don't you leave your mother alone?” At this point the mother, who is mad at the father, turns and says, ”Leave him alone. He hasn't done anything wrong. Besides, this is all your fault. Leave him out of it.” Now the father, who is quite angry, turns to the child and says, “See what you've done. You've made your mother mad.” The mother strongly objects. “Stop it! That's enough!” The mother turns to the child and says, “Honey, why don't you go play in your room?” The child, now very confused, says, “Mommy, why are you mad at me?” The mother says, “Honey, I'm fine. I'm not mad at you. Everything is fine. Run along and play.” And as the child walks away, confused, he can hear his mother angrily lashing out at his father. The child is thinking to himself, I know they’re upset. I can feel that they're upset. Why would they tell me that they're not upset, when I know they are? I don't understand. I guess something inside me is not right. I guess I can't trust my feelings.

That is a logical conclusion and the only conclusion the child can come up with. This is how little by little, we are taught to lose touch with our feelings and to not trust what comes from within. This is how we learn to say what we *don’t* mean. You've often seen that you can’t fool little kids. Why? Because kids are still in touch with how they navigate. They rely on how they feel and how things feel, more than what is said. They can get a very good reading on you and how you are feeling. However, as they grow up, they learn to stop using their feelings to navigate. They also learn to look outside of themselves for guidance, like everyone else does.

Losing track of our internal radar

Let's look at a couple of other ways we lose track of our internal radar. Have you ever heard the expression “The squeaky wheel gets the oil”? Imagine you're in a toy store, minding your own business, walking down the aisles. You come upon the following scene: a small child, maybe five or six, has a toy that he wants. He's picked it up off the shelf, and there's no way he's putting that down. His mother has told him that this is a trip to buy a present for cousin Billy for his birthday, and there is no way he's getting a toy. The little kid is going to be relentless. *I want it, I want it* and the meltdown has begun. The little kids starts to cry, scream, kick, and do everything he can til he gets his toy. Now it's a question of who wears out first, his mother or him. Sometimes the squeaky wheel will get the toy. Unfortunately, this distorts how we navigate. It teaches us that if we have a fit, and we make enough noise and commotion, we will get what we want. However, the universe does not respond to temper tantrums. Sometimes your mother did, but the universe never does. Another way that we lose touch with our navigation is when we're told, if you're good, you will be rewarded for your behavior. Or, if you behave, mommy will buy you an ice cream, or a toy or whatever the bribe may be.

As we begin to lose track of how we navigate or our internal radar, we also lose track of our hunches and intuition. Some people realize that just like our conscience, intuition is also a form of communication. Most people don't know exactly where hunches or intuition are coming from, but they know when they're in tune with it, it feels right and they happily use it. Did you ever notice that when you're feeling good, you have more hunches and intuition than you do when you're not feeling good? Did you ever know who was on the phone before you picked it up? Did you ever have the feeling about something, and it turned out to be right? We learn to ignore our hunches and our intuition. People tell us, don't be silly, you couldn't possibly have known that. Intuition is portrayed in the media as something scary and frightening. There is something freakish about people who are that highly attuned to what's going on around them, and they are strange, scary, and weird. Of course none of that is true, and all of us have hunches, insights, and intuition. Author and psychic Sonia Choquette says, "Our physical senses give us our feet and keep us earthbound, while our sixth sense, gives us our wings and teaches us to soar.

Sadly, few people realize that we have such an important spiritual sense, let alone know how to access or listen to it."[2]

In the last three words of that quote, Sonia is acknowledging that intuition is a form of communication, and you're in tune with this communication when you're feeling good.

Feeling good

When you're feeling good, and your energy is flowing. You're connected to the universe and that's when you want to pay attention to your hunches and insights. I remember one time, two of my brothers and I were downstairs in the family room. We were working on some music, and I remember I had my guitar, a blond-finished 1969 Fender Stratocaster. I was feeling quite good, too. I remember the radio was on. For some reason, we were talking about how good this particular radio station was. I remember it as clearly as if it were yesterday. I said to Johnny and Billy, "This radio station is so good. The next song that they play is going to be *Long Train Runnin'* by the Doobie Brothers." Moments later, the unmistakable rhythm guitar part of *Long Train Runnin'* started to play, and, yes, it did freak them out. Remember, when you're feeling good, you're in the flow, and you can do amazing things. I'm not saying that you'll be able to tell what song will be on the radio next or that you'll be able to guess tonight's lottery numbers. But when you're in the flow, life is wonderful, and good things happen.

Our emotions are communication from our higher selves to our conscious selves. Our feelings are telling us that what we would like is on its way to us, or that we are hindering it. So, our first building block is in place. The first note of our scale is Principle one: **How you feel is important.** When we decide we want something, the universe starts forming energy around it, creating it for us. Our feelings tell us how we are doing. The next part is how does it get to us? How does it manifest in our lives? I'm glad you asked because that's the topic of the next chapter: *the law of attraction.*

---

2 Choquette, Sonia, *Trust Your Vibes, Secret Tools for Six-Sensory Living* Hay House Inc. 2004

Summary:

Your emotions are communication from your higher self to your conscious self.

Your emotions are how you navigate through your life. They are your internal radar.

There are only two emotions: one that feels good and one that feels bad.

All of the good feelings are open, expanding, and flowing. You feel empowered. You're letting all the good things you want flow to you when you feel good.

All of the bad feelings feel confining, constricting, and suffocating. They make you feel like you have no power. They create friction within you and let you know that what you want is being hindered by what you're thinking.

The stronger the emotion is, good or bad, the more important the subject is to you.

You can always change the way you feel by what you think. **Your feelings come in response to your thoughts**. You always have control of what you're thinking.

Society teaches us to guide ourselves from external sources. The best guidance always comes from within.

Losing touch with and/or not paying attention to our feelings can eventually cause major problems in our life, like addictions.

We all have hunches and insights. They are also feelings, which are communications from our higher self. Trust your instincts and follow them.

3

The Law Of Attraction

Principle two says that the law of attraction controls everything. What is the law of attraction? The law of attraction is: things which are the same or similar, are attracted to each other. You've heard the following expressions:

When it rains, it pours,
The rich get richer and the poor get poorer.
As you sow, so shall you reap.
What goes around comes around.

These are all quotations that capture the idea behind the law of attraction. All of these quotes say that what you put out to the universe, you will get back in return and what you get back in return is similar to what you put out. That's why, in our example from principle two, when you start to have a bad day, that bad day usually continues. Why? Because that's what you're putting out to the universe. The same is true when you have a good day. The law of attraction controls everything, and, therefore, is a pretty big law.

There are many laws in the universe like the law of gravity and the laws of motion. However, none of them are as powerful or as big as the law of attraction. Abraham-Hicks says, "The law of attraction is the engine that runs the universe." The law of attraction is running everything in the entire universe by bringing things that are similar together.

Let's look at a real-life example. A number of years ago my wife Marjorie and I had been talking on the phone to a couple in California. We had similar business interests, and we were involved in conference calls together. One time when we were talking we found out we were all going to the same seminar in Phoenix. So, we decided that we would meet and finally connect faces to voices. The plan was that we would get to the seminar early, sit on the right hand side, and try to get into the front row. Whichever couple arrived first would hold two seats for the other. What do you think happened? We all arrived at the exact same time. Marjorie and I came in from one side. The other couple came in from the other side. As we walked up to them, we knew them and they knew us. We all could feel it. You know from reading the last chapter what your feelings are and their importance.

Vibration

Dr. Masaru Emoto, a physicist who studies water crystals, talks about how everything in the universe vibrates. The following quote supports the idea behind the law of attraction and how it "organizes" vibrations in the universe. "It is said that likes attract, and so it would appear that vibrations attract and interact with each other".[3]

Dr. Ervin Laszlo, another physicist who studies quantum physics, has also come across the law of attraction. He says, "The Akashic field conveys the most direct, intense, and, therefore, evident information between things that are closely similar to one and other".[4]

In other words, things that are similar to each other are attracted to each other and come together. Both of these physicists

3 Emoto, Masaru, *Hidden Messages in Water* Translated by David A. Thayne Beyond Words Publishing 2004

4 Laszlo, Ervin, *Science and the Akashi Field. An Integral Theory Of Everything* Inner Traditions 2004

may not call it the law of attraction, but they have both found clear evidence of it working.

You recall in the first paragraph I said you get more of what you put out. Let's take a look at what "putting out" means. All of us are playing a song inside of us, and we are broadcasting it out into the world. At the same time we are also listening to everyone else's song. We are all broadcasting the song that's inside of us, and we are all listening to the songs that everyone else is broadcasting. The song that we are playing inside of us is how we are feeling. It's our current emotional state or mood. I'm also listening to the music that you are playing. So, each of us is always playing a song and always listening to the other songs that are going on around us. The song we're playing in that moment controls what we're attracting. When we're in a good mood and playing a happy song, we're attracting happy things, good things. When we're in a bad mood, playing a sad song, we are attracting things we don't really want. Remember from chapter two, that we can tell what we're doing or what song we're playing, by how we feel.

Think about it. We always know when somebody's mad even if it's someone we don't know. We can "feel" it. We usually can tell when people are happy, sad, or upset. We hear the song that they are broadcasting. At times we try to hide what song is playing inside of us by playing roles and hiding behind masks as we talked about in chapter two. When we try to hide our feelings, all that really does is move us away from how we are feeling and our internal radar. If you pay a little bit more attention, you will easily be able to tell what song people are playing and know if their mood is good or bad. The people, things, and events that are similar to the song that you are playing will be all around you. That's how the law of attraction works.

There is no such thing as "no"

The law of attraction is the engine that runs the universe. It does this by bringing things together. The universe is based on inclusion, which means everything is included, and everything that comes together has been attracted. There is no law of assertion.

Nothing can assert itself into your life. That means the only way something can come into your life is by you attracting it. Now for the tricky part. There is no such thing as "no". Principle three says **the universe always says yes and does not give up on you**. The law of attraction is the reason there is no such thing as no. The universe is a place of inclusion. That means that everything is included. There's no way to remove something from the universe. So when you see something that you want and say yes to it, you're getting it. It's on its way to you. When you see something that you don't want and say no to it, you're still attracting it because you are focusing on it. This is one of the main reasons why we navigate with our feelings; they indicate or warn us when we are trying to say no to something. So when we are feeling bad, the communication is that you don't want this. You're trying to say "no" to it, but you can't, so your higher self is going to let you know what you're doing by your feeling a negative emotion.

What am I supposed to do when I start thinking about something that I don't want? The only thing you can do is change the subject. If you continue to think about what you don't want, it's on its way to you. Have you ever heard someone say that his or her worst nightmare is coming true? Or someone say the thing they feared the most seems to be coming true? That is how the universe works. There is no such thing as fate or coincidence. It's all the law of attraction. That is how the law of attraction works. We have total and complete free will. We can choose the very best or the very worst. It's all up to us. The more we choose the very worst, the worse we will feel. Our feelings are always with us. If we pay attention, we always know if what we're doing is good or bad for us by how we feel. This is a very important point to remember. **There is no such thing as no**. If you're not sure how you are feeling, then pay attention to what you say to people; sometimes what you say can also let you know what song is playing inside of you.

Do you listen to what you say? Do you pay attention to what you say? If you stop and listen to what other people say, you may be quite surprised what comes out of people's mouths. I was in a store, and I went up to the woman to pay for what I was buying. She said to me, "How are you?" I said, "I'm fine, thanks. How are you?" She said, "I don't have my brain screwed in right." I kind of looked at her like what am I supposed to say to that. You can tell what song others are playing by what they say. Also, with a little practice, you will be able to feel more consciously what song they're playing. I can hear the chords starting this song. It has a bit of a country-down-on-your-luck flair to it....

I don't have my brain screwed in right today.
I got bitten by my dog.
The cows have run away.
I forgot to get my...... Everybody, Sing along!
I don't have my brain screwed in right today.

You get the idea.

I know someone at work who complains about bad customers. Obviously, he's never heard the expression *you get what you say.* Wait, I feel another sing-along coming....

I like to complain.
I like to bitch about things.
Bitch, moan, and complain.
Bitch, moan, and complain. Everybody. Sing along!
It's up to you to sing-along or to change the subject.

Changing the subject is the only thing you can do. The universe is based on attraction, and everything is included. If you're attracting something you don't want, and you know you're doing this because you feel bad, then you have to do something about it, because you're the only one who can. If you're someone who is constantly spewing Murphy's Law, then it's time to forget about Mr. Murphy and think about something else. Remember, there is no such thing as no. What you need to do is change the subject. Think about something else.

There is someone I worked with who liked to complain. This was a problem for two reasons. First, I didn't want to hear about it. Second, I didn't want to attract that kind of negative stuff. The rest of our colleagues felt the same way. We all changed the subject whenever this co-worker started up with the negative talk. This person loved to eat and loved to cook, so we would ask him what he had for dinner the previous night. Or, we would ask him about a recipe or how to make something. He immediately went into a detailed explanation of his dinner, and we successfully changed the subject. Most importantly, we all felt better.

Real-life law of attraction stories

Let's look at a few real-life law of attraction stories, so that you can get the idea of how this works. The first story I'm going to tell is about myself. Back then I wasn't quite.... shall we say, as positive as I am now I wanted proof that this worked. The song I was playing inside of me was not very positive, and I was a bit of a smart-ass– you'll get the idea from the story. Marjorie and I were at the beach. This is a place that both of us really like to go. We tend to be a little bit more relaxed and a little bit more positive. We feel better and more of our energy can flow. I decided that I would put this law of attraction stuff to the test. Here we were at a family beach in Maine. I decided that if this really works, I wanted to see a topless woman. As I said, I was a bit of a smart-ass. I figured it was impossible. I would prove once and for all that this didn't work, and we could forget all the studying about positive thinking. We went on about our days doing the usual beach stuff-walking on the beach, looking for sand dollars, swimming, tanning, etc. A few days went by and no topless women. There were plenty of women around, but all of them had their tops securely fastened. Then one morning, the day before we left to return home, I said to Marjorie, "See, this doesn't work at all." No sooner had the words come out of my mouth than a two-year-old topless baby girl ran just a few feet in front of us. We both laughed. I realized this did work, and the universe really is attraction-based. I was being a smart-ass, and the universe showed its sense of humor right back to me.

Here's one that's for all of you. Have you ever bought a new car, and then all of a sudden, that car is everywhere–same make, same model, same color. You don't even have to buy the new car necessarily. You just have to think about buying the car and focus on it, and you'll start seeing it all over the place. It is like they just pop out of the woodwork. I know what you want to say, "Oh, that's just a coincidence." Well, no it's not. It's the law of attraction. There's no such thing as a coincidence.

Here's a "fish"story. It happened a number of years ago, off the coast of Cape Cod. I was out with two of my friends, Bob, who owns the boat we were fishing from, and Jack. We were fishing in the ocean for stripers (striped bass). It was the end of the day, and we decided to troll our way home.

We had two weighted lines off the back of the boat with eight-inch lures on them, running probably about 30-feet deep. Jack, who knows better had thrown his line of mono-filament out off the side and was trolling from there. The reason why you don't troll a mono-filament line off the side, without an outrigger, while trolling other lines off the back is because all the lines will get tangled.

There we were, trolling along, when all of a sudden all three poles hit at once. Bob and I each grabbed a back pole and Jack had his pole in his hands, and we all proceeded to set the hook. For a second, it seemed as if we all had a fish. But after we started reeling in the line, it seemed more likely that we caught the bottom. As we reeled the lines in a little bit more, we realized we had a giant tangle behind the boat. The worst case of line spaghetti we'd ever seen. I got most of the tangled lines into a big pile of spaghetti at my feet and begin to untangle it. As I was doing it, I could swear that every once in awhile, one of the lines in my hands, pulled a little bit. But I was thinking, it's just the drag from the boat that we were still driving home. I continued to untangle while the lines were getting closer and closer to the boat. This time, when the line pulled my hand from in front of me, all the way out to the full extension of my arm, I knew we had a fish. I remember a few expletives were shouted, and I started to pull this fish in by hand. Bob turned off the boat and found the gaffe to get ready to grab the fish. At this point, we were starting to see the fish. It was one of the biggest striped bass I'd ever seen. I pulled this fish all the way in by hand. We were just about to get it, and Bob was bending over with the gaffe. I had the line tight, and I reached down with him.

Suddenly, the fish rolled, turned his head, and spit the lure out. My heart was pounding. I wanted to scream. I wanted to jump in the water after it. I couldn't believe what just happened. The fish was close to four feet long. It was about half the size of the back of the boat, and it just got away. ARGHH!

Okay. You lost a big fish. Big deal. What does that have to do with the law of attraction? Well, I was just getting to that. A year ago I was out fishing with my friend Charlie. We were fishing in the ocean for cod. We were having a slow day. I caught a couple of little fish. He caught a couple of little fish– nothing really to talk about. We started exchanging fish stories. I told him the story you just read. After I finished the story, we decided to hang it up for the day and head for home, and as I started to pull my line up, I got a hit, so I set the hook. I knew it was a big fish. I fought this fish all the way up to the top. It was a nice big cod. The best fish we'd seen in quite awhile. As it was just about to the boat, and we were reaching down to get it, and guess what happened? The fish rolled, turned its head, and spit the hook out. That's right. It got off and swam away. My heart was pounding. I wanted to jump in the water after it. Sound familiar? I learned my lesson. I am never going to tell that fish story again. If someone wants to hear about it they will have to read this book.

Song on the radio

Here's one last story, and, no, it's not another fish story. I was driving home from work on a Wednesday night. The store I worked at closed at 9:00 p.m. I had the radio on, and I was flipping through stations, and I caught the middle of a song that got my attention. It was a song by a woman, and she was singing about remembering to breathe, just breathe. I thought the song was interesting, and I wanted to hear all of it. Then I wanted to know who the artist was that performed the song. I asked the universe right out loud in the car, what's the name of that song and who sings it? I want to hear it again, please.

Well, a week went by, and I didn't hear the song. Wednesday night came around again. I was driving home, and I turned on the radio. I turned to the same station I was listening to the week before. This time the song was playing again, right from the beginning. I heard the whole song, but the radio host never said who sang it. The next night the store closed at 6:00 p.m. I turned on the radio in the car. A different station was playing the song. This time the disc jockey came on the air and said the name of the artist. The next night the store also closed at 6:00 p.m. I heard the song again on a different radio station, and they also said who the artist was. Three nights in a row, on three different radio stations, and at three different times. Yes, I hear you. So what? You heard the song three nights in a row, on three different stations. Well, I'm glad you asked. It was late in November. The song and the album that it is on was not to be released til the following April. There were no copies of it around, and it wasn't being played in heavy rotation on all the stations. As a matter of fact, I didn't hear it again til almost the following May. In the evening of the day that I wrote the preceding paragraph, Marjorie and I were watching TV and a commercial for a new show came on. The music that they were using was the same song I just told you about *Breathe (2 a.m.)* by Anna Nalick, and it was even written there on the TV screen. The next day I had a fairly long drive, and as I was driving I thought to myself wouldn't it be cool if I heard the song. Well, I drove all the way there, and nothing, and I drove almost all the way home and still nothing. I thought to myself, oh well, I guess I'm not going to hear it. Then less than five minutes from home, I pressed the button to change the station, and guess what song was just starting? That's right. Not only did I hear the song, but also I heard the whole thing from start to finish. The song ended as I pulled up to my mailbox. Now are you beginning to understand the law of attraction, or do you still believe in coincidences?

As we conclude chapter three, two more of our building blocks are in place. The second note of our scale is Principle two: **The law of attraction controls everything**. The third note of our scale is Principle three: **The universe always says yes and does not give up on you.** Soon you will be able to play a melody. So far, we've learned that we navigate with our feelings, which is our internal radar. In this chapter we've learned about the law of attraction and that the universe always says yes. There is no such thing as no. The universe is based on inclusion, not exclusion. This brings up a couple of new questions. How does the law of attraction work on everything in the universe? Why are we here? What is the basis of our universe?

Summary:

The law of attraction is the biggest law of the universe.

The law of attraction is the engine that runs the universe.

Things that are the same/similar are attracted to each other.

We are all playing a song inside of ourselves and broadcasting it to the world. The song is how we feel, our mood.

We are listening to everybody else's song all the time.

When we feel good, we are attracting the good things we want.

When we feel bad, we are hindering the things we want from coming to us.

The universe always says yes, and there's no such thing as no. If you say yes to something, you're getting it. If you say no to something, you're still getting it.

The only way to say no is to change the subject.

4

Everything is Vibration.

Quantum physicists have learned that everything in the universe is vibrating. Masaru Emoto says, "I would first like to make sure that you understand this fact: existence is vibration. The entire universe is in a state of vibration, and each thing generates its own frequency, which is unique."[5]

That bears repeating– existence is vibration. Existence means the fact or state of continued being: life. All that exists. Being. I think that covers everything. That means everything is vibration. Masaru goes on to say, "human beings are also vibrating and each individual vibrates at a unique frequency."[6]

Ervin Laszlo talks about everything vibrating together. "They [physicists] see each particle as a string making its own music, together with all other particles. Cosmically entire stars and galaxies vibrate together, as in the final analysis, does the whole universe."[7]

5 Emoto, Masaru, *Hidden Messages in Water* Translated by David A. Thayne Beyond Words Publishing 2004

6 Emoto, Masaru, *Hidden Messages in Water* Translated by David A. Thayne Beyond Words Publishing 2004

7 Laszlo, Ervin, *Science and the Akashi Field. An Integral Theory Of Everything* Inner Traditions 2004

An oversimplified definition of "string theory" is, that everything is made up of tiny particles that are actually little strings and all of these strings vibrate. String theory is a mathematical equation to prove that. In her book *The Field* Lynne McTaggart describes subatomic particles of the universe as follows: subatomic particles weren't solid little objects like billiard balls but vibrating and indeterminate packages of energy that could not be precisely quantified or understood in themselves.[8]

The subatomic particles or strings that make up the universe create a sea of energy. Everything, and I do mean everything, is swimming in this sea of energy and is made from this sea of energy. This sea of energy is referred to as the unified field, the unified vacuum, the quantum vacuum, and the field. Ervin Laszlo refers to it as the Akashic field. Mystics, seekers, sages, masters, medicine men, and shamans have known about this sea of energy for centuries. Some of the other names that refer to it are: Chi or Qi, Prana, Kundalini, Mana, Ni, Num, and Pneuma. Even though string theory is new to science, man has known about the universe being made up of vibration and the sea of energy for centuries.

And everything vibrates

Let's talk a little more about string theory. I am not a quantum physicist, so bear with me. String theory is, and I am paraphrasing here, the theory that the entire universe is made up of small, tiny, string-like particles that interact with each other. How they interact with each other depends on how they vibrate. This is where the law of attraction comes in. Things that are vibrating similarly, or are the same, attract each other. That's how the law of attraction works, and how the law of attraction brings everything together. Everything is vibrating, including people, places, things, thoughts, beliefs, music, art, light, sound– everything. There is nothing in the entire universe that isn't vibrating. I remember being in a high school. The classrooms had fluorescent lights overhead that buzz and hummed. My brother John, an electrical engineer,

---

8 McTaggart, Lynne, The Field. The Quest for the Secret Force of the Universe Quill, 2003 2002 Harper Collins

told me that fluorescent lights vibrate at the same frequency as the musical note B-flat. See how everything vibrates?

Let's look at other examples of how things vibrate together. Our brains tend to "entrain" themselves to frequencies around us. This principle was first expressed in 1665 by Dutch scientist, Christian Huygens, who found that two pendulum clocks mounted side-by-side on the same wall gradually came to swing at the same rate.[9]

When women are together for a while in a group, over time, they all develop the same monthly menstrual cycle. One of my favorite examples of vibration is if you have two guitars, and you put one on a guitar stand, hold the other and pluck a string, the same string on the guitar just sitting there will start to vibrate.

Everything is vibrating. Everything is energy and remains part of and within the sea of energy. Including us. We are much more than our bodies. We are consciousness. We are energy and electricity. Medical science is well aware of the energy inside the body. Every second an electrical impulse tells your heart to beat. Something is creating this energy that sends the electrical impulse. That something is you. You are energy. You are consciousness, and you are vibration. The most obvious example of this is when someone dies. The energy and electricity that was animating the body is gone. I've talked to people who were around others when they've died. Some have noticed an energy moving out of the body that they can feel and sometimes even see. As we all know, when the energy leaves, the body ceases to function. We are all much more than our bodies. Science is finding that the old beliefs that chemical reactions and DNA control our bodies are not true. We are energy. We are consciousness. We are so much more than the flesh and blood that you see when you look in the mirror.

The "songs" we are playing inside of ourselves

Everything is vibrating all the time. It's said that music is the only language where many people can "talk" all at once and all be understood. What we say and our body language makes up

9 From the CD jacket *Brainwave suite*. by the Relaxation Company.

a very small part of our communication. Our vibration, which I've referred to as the song we are playing inside of ourselves and broadcasting, is the biggest part of our communication. Have you ever noticed that you're attracted to certain people and not to others? This has to do with vibrations; you and the person you feel attracted to are vibrating similarly while you and the person you are repelled by are not. Did you ever notice that some people are just very likable and nice to be around? It's because of the way they are vibrating. We say things like, we were on the same wavelength, or we just connected easily. You feel everyone else's vibration, all the time. Whether you'd notice it or not is up to you.

Let's have a quick review. We are swimming in a sea of energy. Everything is vibrating within this sea of energy. Why are we here, and what are we supposed to do? We are here to create. You recall Principles four and five: Y**ou create your own reality,** and **You create your own reality even if you don't know you're doing it**. This is why we are here. Neale Donald Walsch, in his book *Conversations with God,* writes three times before page 50 that "God" says we are here to create. Lynne McTaggart says that every minute of every day, we are creating our world. She goes on to say that at the lowest level of mind and matter, each of us creates the world.[10]

The universe is a massive sea of energy waiting for someone to direct it and waiting for someone to create with. That someone is you, and you're directing and creating all the time, whether you realize it or not. In the previous chapter on the law of attraction, I gave lots of examples about the things that I was thinking about manifesting in my own life. This process happens naturally, all the time, because of the law of attraction and vibration. Now that you're aware of this, you have a choice. You can create on purpose, or you can create by default. If you want to create the life of your dreams, you have to create on purpose. You have to decide what you want to create in your life. It's not hard to do. It just takes some practice, and that's what this book is about.

---

10 McTaggart, Lynne, *The Field. The Quest for the Secret Force of the Universe* Quill, 2003 2002 Harper Collins

Think of yourself as a musical instrument, maybe a piano or guitar. The things and events of your life play or vibrate certain songs within you. Some you like and some you don't. This is creating by default. When you choose your own songs within you, and let the universe match you, this is creating on purpose, or deliberately creating. Catherine Ponder says tremendous vibratory forces can be set up in the invisible [non-physical], profoundly affecting substance and producing results.[11]

She is referring to putting the law of attraction to work for you in creating what you want. The process is fairly simple. Decide what you want, and the law of attraction will bring it to you as long as you and what you want are playing the same song. This means that you are both the same vibration or frequency. Your emotions tell you how you're doing. When you feel good, what you want is easily flowing to you. When you feel bad, you're hindering it. As you can see, the process is not difficult. However, the deciding of what you want and fine-tuning will keep you busy for the rest of your life.

We create all of it

Which feels better to you? Life is a chaotic place. Someone or something is controlling everything, and you have little or no say in it– shit happens. Or, you create your own reality, and you are guided from within. The universe loves you, in both the largest sense and in the most personal way possible.

We've already talked about trying to guide ourselves from the outside. How could anything outside of you possibly know what's best for you? How can anything outside of you know what your vibration is? Are you starting to realize how amazing your feelings are and how accurately they guide you in every single situation, if you pay attention to them. Remember, your feelings are communication from your higher self to your conscious self. They are here to help you assist in your life and in what you're creating. We create our own reality every minute of every day. We are vibrating, and the universe matches our vibrations.

11 Ponder, Catherine, *Open Your Mind to Prosperity* Devorss 1983

I recently was talking to somebody, and this subject came up. I said to him, "You create your own reality". He replied, "Oh I heard something like that recently. Okay, but what part of it do we create?" I replied, "All of it". "What do you mean, by all of it?" "Well, I mean everything, how you feel, where you live, what kind of job you have, how much money you make, the kind of car you have, what food you like, the kind of music you like, how things go for you, whether you're late or on time, all the good things, all the bad things, your health, and I could keep going on. I really mean everything." There was a pause for a moment. He had a look on his face like, I'm sure you have right now, if you haven't heard of this before. It was a cross between the excitement and freedom of the truth, the feeling of relief, and a bit of terror as he realized that he does **create everything in his life**. I have a quote by my desk that reads: "Life isn't about finding yourself. Life is about creating yourself." *(Unknown.)*

Abundance

We have to have access to vast resources in order to create our lives. As I mentioned earlier, the universe is a vast sea of energy. The resources that we need are available to us. The universe is based on abundance. There is more than enough for everyone and then some. We don't have to look too far to find evidence of this. The Bible, which is considered to be a source of knowledge and information, talks about abundance in the universe in the book of Genesis. The Bible says, "In the beginning God created a lavish universe, and created spiritual man and placed him in this world of abundance, giving him dominion over it."[12]

This brings us to principle six.

There is plenty for everybody.

Man has taught himself that there is not enough. If you look around, you will see abundance everywhere. Look at the leaves on the trees. Look at the stars in the night sky. You need to get out

12 Genesis 1.

where it's dark so you can really see the stars. There are millions of them. Have you ever been to a "shelling beach" where there are seashells everywhere? I'd never seen so many seashells in all my life. There were millions of them. Never mind the seashells. Think about the grains of sand on a beach. There are billions and billions of those. I know about the supposed scarcity of natural resources. We are told there are only limited supplies of resources. How could this possibly be true if the universe is based on abundance? The answer is simple: it can't be true. There has to be something else behind it. What's behind it is politics and money. In the book, T*he Soul of Money* Lynne Twist, talks about this very fact. She cites as an example, a quote from Bernard Liether's book, *Of Human Wealth.* Liether says that greed and fear of scarcity are programs. They do not exist in nature, not even in human nature.[13]

Fear of scarcity, which is the belief in lack of abundance, is programmed into us. It has to do with the bigger game of economy and of money and of how people try to control us. Lack of abundance does not exist in our universe. However, if you believe in lack, that's what you will get– even though it has nothing to do with the abundance of the universe. This is a prime example of how the law of attraction works.

The order of the universe is abundance. The universe is inexhaustible, completely unlimited. Abundance is the rule, not the exception. I'm sure if you look around, you can find plenty of examples of the abundance of the universe. How about the abundance of people? What about the rocks in the ground when you're trying to plant your garden? How about the abundance of plants? Did you ever notice that a patch of dirt doesn't stay like that for very long before the plants fill it up? How about the abundance of weeds that seem to come out of nowhere? This all comes down to what you believe. If you believe in lack of abundance, you will never have enough. If you look around and choose to see it, you'll see that there is abundance everywhere.

As we finish up this chapter, we've covered a lot of ground together. We've learned some quantum physics and found out that

---

13 Twist, Lynn, Soul of Money Transforming Your Relationship with Money and Life W.W.Norton & Co. Inc. 2003

everything in the universe vibrates. It's because of this fact that the law of attraction can bring things together. When the song that you're playing inside of you is the same as the song of what you want, then what you want manifests in your life. That is the universal law of attraction. Now that we understand how the law of attraction works, we have quite a few more building blocks in place. We now have quite a few notes for our scale. The fourth note to our scale is Principle four: **You create your own reality**. The fifth note of our scale is Principle five: **You create your own reality, even if you don't know you're doing it**. Now that you know that you are creating your own reality and that you can do it on purpose– or you can do it by default– you have a choice to make. Do you want your life to go according to your plans and your goals? Or do you want to continue to bounce around like a ping-pong ball? It's up to you. The last note in our scale from this chapter is Principle six: **There is plenty for everyone.** The universe is based on abundance. There are examples of this abundance everywhere, if you look for them. It just depends on what you focus on. Let's review our process. We decide what we want. We focus on it. The law of attraction brings it to us. Throughout this process, our emotions tell us how are doing.

Let's talk about focus. What we focus on is what we are paying attention to. "Paying attention to" is another way of saying we are thinking about something. Focusing on something and thinking about something are the same thing. This brings us to our next chapter called *Thoughts.*

Summary:

Everything in the universe is vibration, including us.

The law of attraction uses vibration to match things up.

The universe is a giant sea of energy, and everything is part of this energy.

We are much more than our bodies. We are consciousness and energy.

We are creating our own reality, our own lives.

We are creating our own reality, whether we know it or not.

The universe is made up of abundance and based on abundance.

5

Thoughts

Everything is thought. There's nothing that was not at first created by thought. Think about it. (Very funny.) No, I'm serious. Everything you see was at first a thought. A pen, the car you drive, glasses, the motor in the car, paper clips, anything. There's nothing that you can look at that was not, at first, some sort of thought. A light bulb, a painting, the chair you're sitting in.

Let's talk about that chair. Someone, years ago, sat on a rock and thought, "This hurts my backside and I can't lean back." Thus, the first chair was on its way. The chair-thought has continued to evolve to our modern recliners, high-tech computer office chairs, hydraulic dental chairs, and car seats for all the littlest to the biggest babies. Thought continues to grow and evolve. Think about the modern wonders like the chair we have today and what we are going to see in the future. Everything at first was a thought. As more people think about something that's already been created, it evolves. The thought evolves. The chair might have started from a pile of brush and maybe a bunch of sticks tied together. Then the thought evolved and the modern high-tech chairs were created, with the help of the law of attraction.

The law of attraction works on the thought and brings thoughts that are similar to it together, making it more than it was. In the last chapter, we learned that everything is vibration, including thoughts. Vibration makes thoughts and ideas come together and grow.

Vibrational evolution of music

Think about music and how it started. Primitive music was mostly voice. Banging on things was the birth of rhythm. Someone was tanning a hide that was stretched over something hollow. He hit it and liked the sound it made. Then he thought to himself, "I wonder if..." and the first drums were on their way. Someone found a hollow stick and blew into it, and it made a tone. He may have thought something like, "I can use this to call the rest of my tribe or to scare away animals." From that, the first whistles were on their way. These evolved into wooden flutes, recorders, and eventually the modern woodwind instruments of today. Someone noticed that if you change the tension on a vine or a string, it makes different tones. Someone wondered, what would happen if I stretched it over a stick? From that the first crude stick, stringed instruments were created. Eventually, as more and more people thought about it, the "instruments" evolved into guitars, mandolins, violins, banjos, cellos, and all the modern stringed instruments.

Now we have all kinds of electronic instruments: guitars, basses, keyboards, synthesizers, and drums. We are able to loop sounds together and are able to record sounds and noises and make them into music. Think about the journey of music. From someone banging on something in a cave, to the classical movements and the Renaissance period, to the blues which evolved into jazz. Think about rock and roll and its evolution into punk, glam rock, and heavy metal. Think about techno and disco. Music continues to evolve as more and more people put energy into the thought about music, and that thought grows as the law of attraction joins these similar thoughts together.

Music, for those who may not be familiar with western music theory, consists of 12 notes. From just 12 notes, thoughts, and the law of attraction, music has evolved into what we have today. Maybe major scales came first and then minor scales and that eventually broke off into modal variations. At some point, more than a single note was played at the same time and that was the birth of harmony and chords. Music developed into different keys. As more people thought about it and put more energy into it, more exotic scales were created. Different parts of the world created their own types of music. All of the modern western music that we have today comes from 12 notes. Now imagine what the law of attraction did with 12 notes and think about what it can do with the advanced, complex thoughts that you are able to think right now. I personally marvel at how amazing this is. Thoughts are amazing things.

Are you realizing that all of this, the physical world, started with thought? It was someone's imagination. *I wonder if... How can I? ... What is this like? There has to be a way to do...* For the chair, it was someone sitting on a rock thinking, this hurts my backside. For music, it was someone banging on something with a stick. Look at how far the thoughts have evolved. The physical world all started by thought and imagination. Thoughts are powerful.

The power of thoughts

A thought is an energy form. Thoughts have energy to them; they have sort of an electrical charge. Thoughts are real things. Thoughts are how you create. Your thoughts create your life. You get what you think about. Thoughts are vibrations, just like everything else. When we focus on a thought, after 17 seconds, another thought joins it and starts to create a vortex. "It takes about 17 seconds before it [the thought] begins to register within your vibration."[14]

Physicists call these vacuum Vortices. This is when the law of attraction, using the vibrations of the thoughts, starts to bring

14 Abraham-Hicks excerpt from tape G- 5/3/ 97 Tarrytown New York. The Science of Deliberate Creation quarterly journal and catalog addendum January, February, March 1998 volume 3

similar thoughts together. When we hold a thought for a while, the law of attraction brings thoughts that are similar to it, and they join together. There is a stronger energy surge. You think a thought a little more, you hold it, and think it, and more energy forms around it. Then the law of attraction matches it with another thought that is similar to it. You continue to think it, and the law of attraction matches another thought and another and another and another and that's how, eventually, manifestation takes place. We do not have instant manifestation here. This process does take some time. This is how you create. You create by the thoughts that you think.

Thoughts are very powerful things. We've already talked about the amazing things that have been created by thought. Now let's talk about how thoughts affect you, or should I say how you are affected by your own thoughts. People can do amazing things to their bodies just by using thought. People can completely block out pain by the thoughts they choose. For example, there are people who don't use any Novocain at the dentist. (I am one of them.) I saw a woman on TV getting operated on without any anesthesia. She had worked with a scientist who trained her how to turn off the pain switches in her mind.

Here's another example of how powerful thoughts are. In an article from the Wall Street Journal, scientists studied the brain patterns of Tibetan monks while they meditated. Using the brain scan called functional magnetic resonance imaging, they discovered that the monks are able to alter the structure of their brains.[15]

That's how powerful your thoughts are. They actually changed their brains. You can actually change the physical properties of your body. That's incredible.

Let's play a little game. I want you to think about your favorite food. Whatever that might be, like chocolate cake, moist and rich. You put it in your mouth, and it just sort of melts. You gently chew it and taste the flavor of the chocolate with creamy dark chocolate icing, nice and sweet. Your mouth is having a party. Or maybe you'd prefer a nice piece of pineapple with that beautiful

15 Begley, Sharon, *Wall Street Journal, Science Journal*, November 5, 2004

golden color and that sort of crunchy feel when you bite into it, that sweetness across your tongue and the juices in your mouth. Mmm, isn't that good? Okay, right now, is your mouth watering? I'll bet it is. What caused your mouth to water? The thoughts that you were thinking and nothing else.

Creating with thoughts

Okay, so how do you create with your thoughts? To create with your thoughts your thoughts need to be clear and focused. Thoughts that feel good and are clear and focused with strong desire **are the best**. What does clear mean? A clear thought is a thought that has only one vibration. You recall we talked about playing a song inside of you and broadcasting it to the world. If you are playing more than one song inside of you at once, they cancel each other out. A thought that has more than one vibration has no real power and cancels itself out. The law of attraction matches the thoughts and brings similar thoughts together, and they keep growing, becoming more and more. Eventually, the thoughts manifest in your life. When you're playing two songs inside of you, at the same time, you're sending off a double vibration, which either isn't enough for the universe to match or the universe matches some of both vibrations. You really don't gain any ground and nothing seems to happen.

Focusing on a thought means to think about one subject or thing for 17 seconds or longer. "If you hold your attention to it [the thought] for as little as 17 seconds you begin to vibrate as it is vibrating."[16]

This thought should feel good. You want your thoughts to feel good for two reasons. First, you remember from chapter two that emotions are communication from your higher self. When you feel good, you are letting your energy flow. Second, the law of attraction matches what you're putting out. So, if you're putting out negative, you're going to get back negative. Remember the expressions, *what goes around comes around and as you sow, so shall you reap?* Thoughts that are clear and focused create your life. **You get what**

---

16 Abraham-Hicks *The Science of Deliberate Creation* July, August, September 1998 quarterly journal volume 5

you think about and that's how it works. Things manifest in your life all the time. Innately, you know how to do this. What we are learning here is how to do it on purpose. How to choose your thoughts and what you should focus on so you can manifest the things you want into your life. This is referred to as "creating on purpose".

For example, I want a new guitar (first vibration) but new guitars are very expensive (second vibration). The thought has two vibrations and has no real strength. It's not clear. I want a new guitar because it will be fun to play on. That's a clear, positive thought. I can't afford a new guitar because they're too expensive. That's a clear negative thought. Both are equally powerful.

We need a clear, focused thought. There is desire in it (it will be fun to play on). Remember a key part is how the thought feels. Having a new guitar because it's fun to play is a thought that feels good. That thought fits all of our criteria. The other thought, but it's too expensive, is focused and clear and does have desire, but it's negative and it doesn't feel good. That thought does not fit our criteria. Remember the law of attraction is matching everything. I want a positive happy life and good things that feel good. That is what I want the law of attraction to match. The law of attraction is completely neutral. It'll match either positive or negative as long as the thought is clear and focused. I want to match things that feel good, will be positive, will make me happy, and will enrich my life.

Let's try another example since I'm guessing that not all of you want a new guitar. How about going on vacation? Okay, so we want to create a thought that's clear and focused and has positive desire in it. I love to go on vacation and to get away from it all. It was good, but it's not very specific. Let's try again. I love to go to the beach and walk barefoot on the sand and smell the ocean and hear the sounds of the waves. That was a good one. It's clear and focused and has desire in it, and it's all positive, all one vibration. You may have noticed that I left out the last part of the first sentence, which was to "get away from it all" because that comment was negative.

Now, I will give an example of a thought that has two vibrations. I want to go on vacation and stay at a nice resort, but I don't have enough money. I think you can see that the part about not having enough money is the second vibration and the negative part. The first thought about about a nice resort is the one that the law of attraction starts working on. The second part is another vibration– negative– and it cancels out the first part. The law of attraction works on both parts of that so you get some positive and some negative but no real strength. No real gain. Let's go back to the feeling part again. The first part, I want to go on vacation and stay at a nice resort, feels good. The second part about not having enough money doesn't feel good. You can feel the energy go up on the first part and go down on the second part.

Let's try one more to make sure you're getting it. I know a lot of people are looking for their soul mate, life partner, significant other, etc. Let's look at some thoughts that would help that process and some thoughts that hinder that process:

All of the good ones are taken.
I can never seem to meet the right person.
The single's scene is a meat market.

What do you think about those three thoughts? All of them are clear and focused and negative. They have attracting power, but they're attracting in the wrong direction. If you're thinking thoughts like that, you're actually not attracting what you're looking for, and you're flowing energy away from what you're looking for. When you think the same thought over and over, you create a path in your brain from the neurotransmitters. These neurotransmitters are always firing with the same connections. Have you ever heard anyone say they're in a rut? The neurotransmitters in your brain do create kind of a rut. Einstein said, "One cannot solve a problem with the same kind of thinking that gave rise to that problem."

Let's try some others:

I enjoy meeting people
I meet very interesting people all time.
I know my perfect match is out there somewhere, and somehow, some way, I am going to find them.

Some people really enjoy the single's scene and meet lots of people. It's not the greatest to me, but I'm doing all right.

I feel good about my future knowing that I'll find the right person to share it with.

What do you think about those for thoughts? The first one is good. It has desire. It's clear, focused, and only one vibration. It's a little bit off the subject, but it's still attracting energy in the right direction. The third thought is pretty good, but it's somewhat contradicted. It implies that finding someone is a long arduous task, and it doesn't have to be that way. You probably want to rephrase the thought and make it more like the fun of the adventure.

The next thought also has two vibrations. If you don't enjoy the single's scene then focus your thoughts elsewhere because a contradicted thought keeps you in the same place that you are in right now. The two vibrations cancel each other out, so nothing really changes, and you're not flowing clearly. The best thought of all is probably the last. It has desire, its clear, positive, and focused. The law of attraction is bringing to you what you want when you're thinking this thought. This is how the law of attraction matches up your thoughts and brings the ones that are the same together. One attracts another, and if you keep thinking it, it attracts another and that continues until some point when you get a manifestation. As long as the thought feels good, you're in harmony with what you want. You're focused, clear, and getting what you want. If the thought feels bad, then you know from the feeling that you're off track.

Law of attraction working on thoughts

Here's a good analogy for the law of attraction working on your thoughts. There is a toy that is a little egg. Inside the egg, is a small little foam creature. You put the creature in water and let it sit overnight. The creature is made of foam that absorbs the water. By the time you look at it the next morning, it's 10 or 15 times bigger than it was. It grows as it absorbs the water. This is what the law of attraction does. Once you get an energy vortex started around the thought, then the law of attraction keeps working on it, and it keeps growing. When we keep thinking the thought, it keeps getting bigger and bigger, attracting more and more, and, eventually, it will manifest. The law of attraction is like sunlight for plants. Whatever thoughts you put in the "sunlight", the law of attraction "nurtures" and causes them to grow.

Let's look at how the law of attraction nurtures our thoughts. If we look up the word *think* in a thesaurus, this is what we get; contemplate, ponder, concentrate, focus on, study, analyze, consider, evaluate, reflect, deduce, reason, conceive, imagine, picture, and remember. Whenever we engage in any form of thinking from the previous list, we are playing a song inside of us. We are creating a vibration. The law of attraction is completely neutral. It simply matches the vibration that we are sending out, when we are thinking it. We can think about the past, present, or the future. Each creates a different vibration within us. We also create vibrations within us by the activities that we are doing. When we are reading a book, our vibration becomes a combination of our thoughts and what the book is saying. When we are watching a movie or TV program, our vibration becomes a combination of our thoughts and what we are watching. This is true of any activity that we do. Whatever we give our attention to, we get that back. **You get what you think about.** When you're listening to music, you're sending off a vibration of the music that you're listening to, and the law of attraction will bring you more. This is why our feelings are so important. They are letting us know what we are giving our attention to. I think you're beginning to understand that thoughts are very powerful. When you link it with your focused attention, the law of attraction joins it. Now it's a powerful tool for creating.

Thought vs action

Because the power of thought, and how the law of attraction works with it is not generally known, we are taught to try to do things using activity and action. When we understand the power of thought and energy, we will realize that using action is not the most effective way. Catherine Ponder in her book, *Open Your*

Mind to Prosperity writes, "It has been estimated that success may be as much as 98% mental preparation and only 2% outer action."[17]

Whether she called it the law of attraction or not, that quote illustrates that she understood the power of thought, versus the power of action. You can see by using her ratio of 98% to 2% that the power of action is minute compared to the power of thought. You also recall from the beginning of this chapter all the amazing things that have been created by thought and just how powerful thought really is. Let's look at how we use action and how it is not the most effective way to get what you want.

An action world

We live in a world that's predominantly based on doing, action, and activity. We believe the best way to get things is by using action and activity to get us what we want. When I was working at the rug store, the boss would come in and ask us if we are busy. Then he would go to check the book to see how many sales we made. Sometimes he would get concerned because there would be a lot of people and a lot of activity but not a lot of sales. He was obviously mistaking activity for productivity. Action, doing, and activity do not guarantee success. Action and activity do not equal productivity. Doing, doing, doing, action, action, action, no wonder people are so tired. No wonder people want to quit the "rat race". Action and doing don't have anywhere near the power of thought. Do you remember the joke about wanting to be a human being instead of a human doing? If you use your thoughts to create what you want you can go back to being a human being instead of a human doing. Instead of the hamster caught on the wheel running, running, running you can be living. We have been taught to "do" and how to use our action and activity instead of our thoughts. I've often said we need to use our brains not our backs. As we learn how powerful our thoughts really are, action will become the second step. Now that you know how powerful your thoughts are and how the law of attraction works with your

17 Ponder, Catherine, *Open Your Mind to Prosperity* Devorss 1983

thoughts, you can use your thoughts to create what you want. Remember, 98% thinking and 2% doing.

To boldly go...

Suppose we lived in a world where everything we thought came to be. Whenever we were thinking about whatever we wanted, it came to us. Wouldn't it be a good idea to think positive thoughts? In one episode on the original TV show *Star Trek* the crew came upon a planet and, as usual, they had to go down and explore it. The planet was beautiful and looked a lot like Earth. While on the planet, somehow, whatever they thought about miraculously appeared. One of them thought about a girlfriend he knew from years ago, and all of a sudden, there she was. One of them was talking about an enemy airplane from World War II, and the next thing they knew, it was in the air flying above them. Then they said, we would probably be fine as long as the airplane didn't shoot at us. With that, the plane turned and fired upon them. What was happening was most of the crew members were having negative thoughts and negative expectations, and they were getting kind of banged up. As it turned out, the aliens who inhabited the planet went and took the crew and patched them up and got them back to health. Then Dr. McCoy came back to explain to Captain Kirk that the whole premise of the planet was that you could have anything you wanted. You just had to think about it, and it would come to you. As long as you thought positive, happy things everything would be fine. At the end of the show, they explained that to the crew then gave them shore leave on the planet. The planet was sort of an amusement park for modern space travelers who could control what they thought about.

Wouldn't it be interesting if there were a planet like that, and that could really happen? Well, there is. That's what this planet is. Everything you think you create. We are here to create. Remember Principle four: **You create your own reality**. You are creating your own reality with the thoughts that you think, combined with the law of attraction. We now have another building block in place. The next note of our scale is Principle seven: **Thought is**

everything and everything is thought. This entire chapter has been talking about the power of thought and how you create with it. **The most powerful thing in your life is the thoughts that you think.** We almost have all the notes to our scale, and soon we'll be creating the music of our lives and playing it the way we want to. I've shown you the awesome power of your thoughts and that thought is everything and everything is thought. Now I am telling you the most powerful of all is what you believe. Your beliefs are more powerful than your thoughts. However, your beliefs are a product of your thoughts. Curious? Do you want to know how that works? That's the topic of our next chapter.

Summary:

Everything is thought. Everything is created by thought.

Thoughts are powerful. A thought is an energy form.

You use thoughts to create.

You get what you think about.

Your thoughts create your life.

Thoughts that are clear, focused with strong desire, and feel good are best.

One vibration, 17 seconds, and feels good.

Action, doing, and activity are not as powerful as thinking. First, set what you want in motion with your thoughts, then follow-up with activity, doing, or action.

6

Beliefs

The life you are now living is created by your beliefs. What you believe is the foundation that everything else is built on. Wait a minute Ed, I thought you said thoughts are everything? Thoughts *are* everything. Your entire life, your world is made up of your thoughts. However, thoughts are the building blocks of beliefs, and beliefs are the building blocks of your life. What you think creates your beliefs. Since beliefs are so important, maybe we should take a closer look at them, starting with a definition of beliefs.

A belief is simply a thought that you repeat over and over. Beliefs are like physical habits. Habits are conditioned responses to specific situations, situations you find yourself in over and over. For example, you learned how to walk by finding yourself in the situation of standing on your feet and having no one to support you. You took a step or two to steady yourself, and repeated this over and over til you mastered it. Then, you formed a belief that you could walk. A belief can also be something that was repeatedly said to you by others. For example, if you are told repeatedly as a child that you are smart, you probably will develop a belief that says, "I am smart." If you are told something negative repeatedly, like, "You're stupid" chances are you will develop a negative belief about yourself. If you have negative beliefs, there is no need for concern because beliefs are changeable.

Beliefs are not cast in stone. They are not permanent or unchangeable. In fact, they are very changeable; a belief is really a mental habit, or thought, repeated over and over, and we already know thoughts can be changed. Most people don't take the time to look at their beliefs and decide whether they are working for them or not. A lot of things that you believe about yourself and the world around you were told to you as a child, and you didn't question them. A lot of the things you learned work very well for you in your life, and there's no need to question them. *Everything always works out for the bes*t is an example of a belief that probably works well in your life. Beliefs that work are fine, but beliefs that aren't working for you should be changed. In this chapter, we are going to learn how to change them. Let's take a look at some negative beliefs that people have.

Negative beliefs

One belief that a lot of people have is: *Food is love.* This is not really a helpful belief, especially if you're overweight. A belief that might be more helpful would be something like, *everything I eat is metabolized into energy.* Another belief that most people have is: *As we move through time, our bodies break down.* This is not a helpful belief either. It's also not necessarily true. The basis of this belief is that our bodies are machines, and eventually the machine breaks down or wears out. The things that cause the body to wear out are much more about lifestyle choices, diet, stress levels, and things like that. That is not the same as your body breaking down simply because it's moving through time. I, personally, prefer the philosophy of agelessness.

Speaking of aging, with age can come wisdom. I remember once being part of a conversation where an older, wiser man said to a young man, "The only mistake you made was believing someone when they told you that you were stupid." The older man went on to prove to the young man that he was not stupid at all. However, the young man had always believed he was stupid because of what he was told as a child. You are what you think, your thoughts are everything, and thoughts that you repeat become your beliefs. You carry your beliefs with you out into the world wherever you go. The older man told the young man he was not stupid, but because of the young man's deep belief, he still believed that he was stupid. What he needed to do was change his thoughts so he could change his belief. I will discuss changing your beliefs a little later.

Our beliefs are our filters

We live in a world full of stimulation and information, much more than our conscious minds can handle at once. If we try to assimilate all the information our senses pick up, we would probably overload our circuits, so we need some sort of filtering system. Our subconscious or higher self does pick up and assimilate all the information. Our higher self always knows exactly what's going on and where we are. It's our conscious mind that needs the filters. Our beliefs are our filters. Author Barry Kaufman says, "We are in charge. We are the architects of our attitudes and experiences. We designed the world by the way we choose to see it."[18]

So, for example, if one of your filters is, "I like baseball", you will notice a whole lot more things about baseball because the law of attraction will bring you more things about baseball than someone who doesn't like baseball. Their filter may be about gymnastics or ice-skating. Maybe their filter is not about sports at all, in which case they would have very little "sports information" in their life because they filter it out. Now, if they meet somebody that they really like, and this person likes sports, they will probably change their filter and allow some sports information into their life.

Your belief filters can also be, at times, your inner critic or your conscience. Let's look at the following example. Have you ever done a brainstorming session where you deliberately try to come up with ideas for a specific purpose? Have you ever been mulling something over and then had that flash of intuition? An "aha" moment? A spark of inspiration? You feel an energy surge, a jolt

---

18 Kaufman, Barry Neil, *Happiness Is a Choice*, Fawcett Columbine 1991

of happiness and joy. This is pure energy. You've connected with infinite intelligence, your higher self, and you've gotten back an inspiring answer from the universe. Now, what's the next thing you do? You run this idea through your beliefs. For example, when I was writing this book, I liked the idea of using quotes. First, I found a quote I liked, and then I ran it through my inner critic and started asking questions. Does this fit with the chapter? Are people going to understand the connection? Does the quote illustrate the right ideas? If the answer to those questions was no, I'd continue to look. When you do something like that, your beliefs are not only just your filter but also your inner critic.

At other times, your beliefs are your conscience. Your conscience is communication from your higher self. As you run a thought through your beliefs, if it's compatible with what you believe, it will feel right to you. If it's not compatible with what you believe, it will feel inappropriate. This is another example of how your belief system acts as your filtering system. The problem occurs when your filtering system is full of limiting beliefs. When the things you were told as a child become a voice in your head that you continue to say to yourself over and over, this is referred to as self-talk. You are here to create, and you can create anything you want. You are only limited by what you believe. The good news is at any point in your life, you can change what you believe. Remember, you get, and live, what you believe.

How beliefs get started

Okay, you're beginning to understand that you're living what you believe. How did you end up with all these beliefs and what do you do about them? Well, it started when you were a baby. We came into this life as powerful energy beings, knowing who we were and what we were. However, we were also small and helpless and couldn't possibly survive without the help of others. As we started to gain our balance and started paying close attention to the world around us, we began to pick up things from our environment.

Did you ever see a two-year-old interacting with slightly older children? If the older children are sitting on the floor playing with their toys, as soon as the two-year-old gets a moment, she's making a beeline for those toys, much to the chagrin of the older children. The little one wants to do what the others are doing. She can't wait to jump in, get her hands on the toys and try to copy what the older children are doing. Much of what we learn when we are children is by mimicking the people around us. We also copy their vibration, and that's what heredity really is, the picking up of the vibrations of the people around us, our family or whoever we spend a lot of time with. This is where the expression t*he fruit does not fall far from the tree* comes from. We see examples of this all the time: My grandfather was a fireman. My father was a fireman. My uncles are fireman. I'm going to be a fireman. Or, my grandmother was a painter. My mother was a painter. I'm a painter. We have been around our family's vibrations so much that it feels natural to us to do what they do.

Limiting beliefs

The following beliefs may ring a bell inside of you. If any of them do, you may have that belief or something very similar to it within your belief system. These are examples of "limiting" beliefs or beliefs that stop you from doing something that you either want or would like to do. The intent here is to see if you have any of these limiting beliefs in you and to give you an opportunity to change them. Here are some examples:

Food is love.
There is a right way of doing things.
Mistakes are bad.
Love has to be earned.
It matters what other people think.
Struggle is good.
You are what you do.
You need someone else's permission to do what you want.
Money doesn't grow on trees.
The rich get richer and the poor get poorer.
Money is the root of all evil.

A good example of beliefs about money, especially for this chapter on beliefs, is the story of Donald Trump. Donald Trump created a financial empire in New York because he believed he could. Then he seemed to lose everything. However, the one thing that he did keep was his beliefs. That alone was enough for him to make a comeback. Once again, he is one of the richest men in the world. Did you get that? Did you follow that it was what he believed and nothing else? What you believe is the foundation of your life. I'm simply going to say that most people's strongest or dominant belief about money is that there is not enough. I recommend you take a look at your beliefs about money and decide if you should change them.

An example of a negative belief that I had to change in me was that I paid too much attention to what other people thought. This controlled me, and I decided to stop living my life worried about this for many reasons. Here's a real important one: What others think is 99.9% about themselves. All this time you spent worried about what other people were thinking, they were really only thinking about themselves. Let's take a look at this. Let's take an imaginary art class together.

Let's say we're in art class, and there are 10 of us. We are all going to draw a simple still life of a bottle, an apple, an orange, and a basket. We will all stand on the same side and draw it from pretty much the same spot. What should the result be? Well, the result should be 10 drawings that look the same. However, that's never the case. All 10 drawings will look different because each of us has our own style, our own perspective, and our own way of seeing things. Most importantly, we have our own way of thinking– our own filters and beliefs.

Let's take a look at how the knowledge of people having their own filters and their own way of seeing things can be used in police work. My father, who is a retired New York City police officer, told me that when they talked to witnesses, they would get very different stories from the people who saw the event. He went on to say that what they would do is ask someone with glasses if the suspect was wearing glasses. They would ask a well-dressed woman, what type of clothes the suspect was wearing. They would ask the man who was losing his hair, what the suspect's hair looked like. They would ask someone who was heavy, if the suspect was heavy or not. The more witnesses they could find, the more people with different filters they would have access to, and they would get a much clearer composite of the perpetrator this way. This is a great illustration of how people think mostly about themselves.

How do you accept a compliment? When someone says you look nice, do you say, "Oh, this old thing?" Or, "Really? I think I look a mess." Do you say some self-effacing thing, or do you accept the compliment and say, "Thank you very much."? How limiting are your beliefs about yourself?

Sand dollars

The following story is an illustration of how beliefs affect your life. My wife, Marjorie, and I love to go to the beach for vacation and look for sand dollars, shells and things of that sort. The prized possessions by far are the sand dollars. Recently, we decided to go to a different beach in Maine, you know the one I'm talking about, the one with the topless baby running around. On our first day out, we walked the beach. As I was looking around, I saw that there were areas of rocks– lots of rocks– anywhere from the size of small pebbles to about as big as a person's foot. In the past, when I had been on beaches that had lots of rocks, like this one, I usually didn't find whole sand dollars. As we continued to walk, we saw pieces of broken sand dollars, but no whole sand dollars. I said to Marjorie, "We are probably not going to find any sand dollars on this beach because sand dollars and rocks don't mix."

The next day as we were walking, we saw a little girl, probably seven or eight- years-old. She was obviously very happy and enjoying what she was doing. We both noticed her quite a ways down the beach. She had a bucket, and whatever she was looking for, she was finding quite a bit of because she was bending down often, picking things up and putting them into her bucket. When our paths crossed, she turned to us, and with a big smile said, "Hello." After returning a greeting to her, I said, "What are you looking for?" She said, "Sand dollars." I asked her, a little surprised,

"You find sand dollars on this beach?" You know how enthusiastic children can be, she said, "My most favorite thing to find is sand dollars, and I find them here all the time. I've been here all week, and I've been finding lots of them." Then she said, "Wanna see," and showed us a bucket full of sand dollars. We talked a little bit more, and then she was on her way to find more sand dollars. Within a minute of talking to this little girl, I found my first sand dollar. Marjorie found one shortly after that. As our week continued on that beach, we found plenty of sand dollars. What changed? What happened? Obviously there were plenty of sand dollars on this beach, and equally obvious, Marjorie and I were completely blind to them because we believed we wouldn't find any sand dollars. The moment our beliefs changed, we found sand dollars. Author Barry Kaufman says, "Change the beliefs and the resulting feelings and behaviors change."[19]

Judging from this story, your eyesight can change too.

Have you ever tried to find something that was lost? Like your car keys? They are usually sitting someplace right out in the open, under your nose. You are completely blind to them as long as you believe they are lost.

30 Days to a New Belief.

You can change any belief that you want in 30 days. According to many self-help books I've read, it takes 21 days to form a habit. So, I'm giving you nine extra days to make sure you really change the belief. This way if you miss a day or two you'll still be fine. On every single subject there is, you have a belief. The ones that keep coming up, and bother you are the ones that you should change. Those are the ones that are active and the law of attraction is working on. These beliefs are the ones that you are attracting more of to yourself.

Affirmations are a great way to start to reprogram how you think. There are lots of affirmations out there in various books and other media. I'm also going to give you a few to help you get started. However, the ones that you create yourself, that have an

19 Kaufman, Barry Neil, *Happiness Is a Choice*, Fawcett Columbine 1991

energy boost for you, that give you that "aha" feeling are the best. We will get to them in just a minute.

When I was starting out in sales, I had no training whatsoever. The company I started working with had some training but also encouraged us to learn on our own. I started studying sales techniques and how to close the sale. One of the closes I came across was called the Ben Franklin close.[20]

Some of you may be familiar with it. Basically, it goes something like this: When you get to the point in the sale when you are ready to start making the close, you turn to your client and say, " Franklin was considered to be one of the smartest men of his time, and if something was the right thing to do, he certainly always wanted to do it. You feel the same way, don't you?"

Then you would take a piece of paper and draw a line down the center and put a plus sign (+) on the top of one side and a minus sign (-) on the top of the other. You would go about listing all of the positive things, all of the pluses, on one side. Then, you would shut up and let him try to come up with any negatives. When he finished, you would count up all the positives as compared to the negatives. Now, a good salesman can easily come up with way more positives than the client can come up with negatives. You would say, for example, "There are 10 positive points, compared to two negative points. Obviously this is a good idea and this is something that you should do." Then you would proceed with the close of the sale.

Now I hear you, what does this have to do with beliefs? This is the very method we are going to the use for you to create your affirmations. However, just like a good salesman does not help the client with the negative side, you will not write down any negatives. What you're going to do is take a piece of paper and write only the positives, and these will be your affirmations.

It's important that when you sit down to do these, you're in a good mood. Remember, the law of attraction is always at work. If you're in an angry mood or are not feeling good, it is not the time to do this. I suggest before you get started you do something that makes you feel good. It'll certainly help. Maybe listen to some music that makes you feel good and lifts your spirits. If you know

---

20 Hopkins, Tom, *How to Master the Art of Selling* Warner Books 1982

how to meditate, try meditating before you start. (We will talk about how to meditate in chapter sixteen, *Exercises.*) Do whatever you can to be in a good mood, and then start this work. I also have to say that this does take some effort. Try to be inspired by the thought of how your life will change. When your beliefs change, you will start attracting different things into your life.

Let's do one together to get started. How about the subject of money and abundance? That seems to be something a lot of people really want. Get a piece of paper and write across the top of it, "Positive Things About Money." Or, if you like, "Positive Things About Having Money." Here we go:

Money is good.

I like having money because when I have money, I can buy things.

Okay, those two aren't bad, but how do they feel? Are they resonating with you? Do they make you feel good? Let's try to find a few more that really feel good:

I love buying the things that I like.

I feel really good sitting in a brand-new car.

I love walking into a house, knowing that it's mine.

I feel eager and proud that it's my house.

The last three may seem like they were a bit off the subject. But they weren't, and the important thing about those three is that they really started to bring feeling into it. Remember we were talking about the law of attraction and feelings. A good feeling is really important. Now suppose we thought about a few negative things as we were going along. That's fine. We just don't pay attention to them, don't write them down, and keep thinking of better ones.

The key to this is to keep going and list as many as you can, and pay attention to the ones that feel the best. Put a star or an asterisk next to the ones that feel really good. Then, on a separate piece of paper, write down your starred choices. However many you have are fine, these are going to be your affirmations. For the next 30 days as many times during the day as you can **and still feel good**, you're going to repeat these affirmations to yourself. As you do, you want to try to get that good feeling to come back to you, that "aha" that came when you thought them. Just think about them for 30 seconds here and there. If you consistently do this, you will change your beliefs. You're also going to find that it doesn't take 30 days to really change what you believe.

Work on one belief at a time

I suggest you only do one belief at a time. As the new energy starts to flow, your old beliefs will start to fall away. Sometimes life can get a little hectic. If this starts to happen, just back off a little bit. Give it a rest for a few days and then start again. This is not an excuse not to do this or to stop doing it. As I said earlier, it does take a little bit of effort.

Let's try another one just for fun. Let's do "Things I Like About My Body." I know that this is also a big one for a lot of people. If you think your body is not in the shape you want it to be, then don't pick your whole body. Pick something on your body that you like and focus on that. For example (remember we want it to feel good):

I have beautiful blue eyes.

I like that I'm tall.

I have beautiful hands, and I love the way they play my musical instruments.

I like the color of my hair.

All of those are good and all of those have good feelings behind them. Let's try to dig in a little deeper, really reach for things that feel good.

I love waking up in the morning and feeling refreshed.

I love the feeling after I have eaten a good, healthy meal.

As you get on a roll with these and start to feel really good, you can put in a new belief at this point. You might say my body metabolizes everything I eat into energy. That could be a new belief to help reprogram your psyche.

This is how you would do that in your day-to-day practice of your affirmations. You would say all the ones on your list that you starred. You would notice that you're feeling better. Then you would state your new belief. The affirmations that you're saying are the start of your new belief. If you want to add something else to it, that would be the way to do it.

Here are some affirmations to help you get started.

I am worthy as I am right here right now.
I appreciate and approve of who I am right here right now.
I am creating my own life all the time.
I'm excited about my life and all that's before me.
Abundance is the natural state of the universe and of my life.
There is more fun coming.
I love to feel good.
Everything I eat, my body metabolizes into energy.
I am safe and the world is a safe place.
Money flows easily to me.
Money is good, and I like having it.
I am completely unlimited.
It's all up to me. I am creating my life.
I can be anything I want, I can do anything I want, I can have anything I want.
How I feel is important, and I want to feel good.
I've decided to feel good.

I hope you find those affirmations helpful, and I hope you take the time to create some for yourself, because the ones that you create for yourself will be much more powerful and have a bigger impact on your life than ones I give you. As we conclude this chapter, we have almost all of our building blocks in place. The next note in our scale is Principle eight: **The life you are now living is what you believe.** We now have talked about our first eight principles, which make up the notes of our scale. The rest of the chapters with the exception of chapter fourteen, are all fine-tuning. Chapter fourteen, Self-Worth is another building block. Now we have our scale notes, and we're ready to play the music of our lives. How do we do that? I'm glad you asked, because "asking" is the subject of the next chapter.

Summary:

Your whole life is built on your beliefs.

Beliefs are thought habits.

Your beliefs are how you filter the world.

It's not hard to change your beliefs. They are not cast in stone. They are not permanent.

Heredity is your family's vibration, but you can change it.

If a belief keeps coming up, or is getting in your way, you may want to change it.

99% of what people think is about themselves.

You can create your own affirmations and use them to change your beliefs.

7

Ask

If we look up the word "ask" in the dictionary, one of the definitions is "to make a request". If we look up the word "desire" in the dictionary the definition is "a request". In this book, ask and desire, mean the same thing. Asking is a request. The interesting thing about asking is this: To ask for something, you have to think about it. We know from chapter five that thoughts are an energy form. Asking is a thought form. We also know that when we hold a thought for 17 seconds, the law of attraction gets hold of that thought and starts matching it up with other thoughts. We know from chapter four that everything is energy and vibration. This sums up the basic concepts that we have learned so far.

Let's look at how asking, energy, and vibration come together. In chapter four you learned that we are swimming in a giant sea of energy, and everything is made up of energy. We use this energy to create our lives. This energy contains infinite intelligence, and is the life force that animates everything. This energy is for us to direct. As quantum physicists study the tiny particles of the universe, they have noticed that the particles don't take on any solid form until someone directs these particles. The particles are existing in several potential states at the same time. They have no definite characteristics until they are observed or measured. The act of measuring or observing the particles pulls them out of the potential states and makes them real.

What that means is all this energy is sitting there waiting for someone to direct it. Once it's directed, it moves from a state of "potential" into a state of "being". This is the very heart of three of our principles. Principle two: T**he law of attraction controls everything.** Principle four: **You create your own reality.** Principle five: **You create your own reality, even if you don't know you're doing it.** You create your own reality by asking. When you ask, you are directing the sea of energy to create what you're asking for. You already know that the law of attraction is the engine that does this by matching vibrations.

Now here's the exciting part. The energy of the universe is all around us, just waiting for someone to decide what to do with it. Guess who gets to decide? You do. You decide by asking. What you ask for directs the energy of the universe. There are two types of asking. The first is asking for something. This can literally be anything. A car, a book, money, an event to transpire, your flight being on time– anything. The second type of asking is for information, which we talked about in chapter five. I wonder if... how do I do this? I want information about____________. The sea of energy also contains infinite intelligence, which you have access to simply by asking.

The strength of desire

The other part of this is the strength of your asking. How badly do you want "it"? How strong is your desire? The stronger your desire, the stronger your asking, and the stronger that you ask, the more energy you pull through you. This is where your feelings come into play. They let you know how you're doing. When you're pulling more energy with your desire than you currently believe is true, you are not letting all of the energy you're asking for flow, and you feel bad. For example, if you want a million dollars, that's fine, til you decide you want it by Friday. Your current belief filter tells you that there is no possible way for you to get a million dollars by Friday. Physically, you would feel bad. If you continue to have a very strong desire about getting the money, but continue to hold the belief that it's impossible, the imbalance of energy flow within you might create a headache, stomachache, or some other ailment in your body. Did you just realize why it's important to know what your beliefs are and how to change them if necessary? The strength of your feeling also corresponds to how strongly you're asking for something.

You are asking all the time, whether you know it or not, which is Principle five: **You create your own reality, even if you don't know you're doing it.** All of us are asking continuously, not just us (our consciousness) but our bodies, too. For example, do you ever feel hungry or thirsty or feel like you need to sleep? That is your body asking. Your consciousness (you) is also asking all the time, by your vibration, by the thoughts that you think, and sometimes by the words that you speak. When you see something and you think, "I like that," you're asking. When you feel cold and want to be warm, you are asking. As I said, we are asking machines. We are asking all the time, and we couldn't stop asking even if we wanted to. That's the way the sea of energy works and how we create by asking.

The universe always answers

It's the universe's job to answer us. The universe always does, and the universe always says yes. This is Principle three: **The universe always says yes and does not give up on you.** Remember, this is a universe of inclusion. There is no such thing as "no" here. You are getting everything that you're asking for. Even if it's something you don't want. If you're giving your attention to it, you're asking for it. Remember, there is no law of assertion. Nothing can force itself into your life. You have to ask for it.

One of the most important quotes about asking comes from the Bible. "Ask and it shall be given you; seek, and ye shall find; knock, and it shall be opened unto you:[21] for every one that asketh,

21 Matthew 7: 7, Luke 11; 9,10; John 14:13 *The bible*, King James Version Thomas Nelson Inc 1976

receiveth; and he that seeketh findeth; and to him that knocketh, it shall be opened."[22]

The first thing that happens is you ask, which directs the energy, and then the law of attraction starts matching it up. The universe can answer you specifically, and give you what you're asking for. The Bible goes on to say, "or what man is there of you, whom if his son asked bread, would give him a stone?[23]

Or if he asks a fish, will he give him a serpent?"[24]

The second part of the quote from the Bible explains Principle three: **The universe always says yes and does not give up on you.** The universe always says, "Yes, you can have exactly what you want." But, you have to be the same general vibration of what you want in order for the law of attraction to get it to you. Remember earlier we were talking about clear thoughts? I want this, but it's too expensive. This is an unclear thought. You asked, the universe replied, but you're not the same vibration of what you want. So, it seems like you don't get what you want.

The energy of the universe flows through us, as we direct it by asking for what we want. Here's an example that will hopefully make this clear. Take any musical instrument, I am going to choose guitar because that's what I play. Just pick up the guitar and start playing. However, if the guitar is out of tune, it's not going to sound good. Asking and not being the same vibration or frequency of what you're asking for is like playing on an out of tune guitar. Because you don't believe you can have what you're asking for, your belief filters are blocking the energy from flowing. You're out of tune with your desire. When we were talking about clear thoughts earlier, you recall that a clear thought contains one belief and one vibration. This single focus allows the energy flow. An out of tune thought or an unclear thought contains two contradictory beliefs or two vibrations, and they cancel each other out. You can always tell when you're out of tune by the way you feel. Let's go back to the musical instruments to further illustrate this concept.

---

22 Matthew 7: 8, Proverbs 8: 17 *The bible*, King James Version Thomas Nelson Inc 1976

23 Matthew 7: 9 *The bible*, King James Version Thomas Nelson Inc 1976

24 Matthew 7: 10 *The bible*, King James Version Thomas Nelson Inc 1976

Your orchestra

Remember I said you were more like an orchestra, full of many musical instruments, not just one guitar. Can you imagine the discord of your entire orchestra being out of tune? Occasionally you might hear some music, which would be the same as getting what you're asking for. However, most of the time, you would just get a lot of really bad sounding noise. This is also referred to as being in and out of balance with your energy flow. This is why most people who don't know how to get what they want try everything: praying, begging, crying, working hard, being good, temper tantrums, doing what they're told, and/or bending over backwards to please other people. These people are jumping from song to song to song, not clear, not focused, not in tune. More like a ping-pong ball. They seem to have things manifest all over the place and not know how or why. When you are in tune, you are in balance. Everything that you want is flowing easily to you. When you're out of tune, you are out of balance. Some of the energy is flowing, but not easily.

In or out of tune

Okay, so how do we know when we're in tune? Remember back in chapter two? Your emotions are how you navigate. When you feel good what you want is flowing to you, your energy is flowing. You are in tune. When you don't feel good, you're not in tune. Your orchestra is playing out of tune and not letting your energy flow. You have to be in tune with what you're asking for. Otherwise, you don't get it. Being out of tune with what you're asking for creates friction in your vibration and frequency. The more you want something, the stronger you are asking for it, and the more energy you are pulling. If you're out of tune with what you're asking for, you're creating friction in your frequency.

Let's talk about friction. Back in chapter two we talked about a car engine with no oil in it. When you want something and you don't believe you can have it, you're creating friction in your vibration. You can feel the discomfort, the friction. If you want something and mostly believe you can have it, this is like driving your car with no oil for only a short distance. You might feel a little bit of friction, but not much. If you want something, and you don't fully believe you can have it, then this would be like driving your car for a medium distance. After a short while, you would definitely know that something is wrong with the engine. You would definitely be feeling the friction. If you want something really strongly and believe you **can't** have it, this would be like driving your car with no oil very fast for a long distance. If you know anything about engines, you know that if you tried to do this, the engine would cease very quickly. The amount of friction would be very large, and you would feel major discomfort. Remember our example about wanting a million dollars by Friday, and getting a headache from that? By changing your beliefs, you balance your desire with the energy flow and get yourself in tune with what you want. Another way of saying this is: When you are vibrating what you want, the law of attraction is matching your vibration.

Once you are in tune with it, what you want will manifest. Remember Principle three: **The universe always says yes and does not give up on you** and what you have asked for? What you want is there for you, as soon as you get in tune with it. It will manifest, even if it takes 86 years.

86 years of desire

The following story is a great example about the strength of desire and getting in tune with that desire. In the year 1918, the Boston Red Sox won their fifth world champion series title, more than any other team had won at the time, including the Yankees. In 1919, Babe Ruth was sold to the Yankees. This is what started the famed "curse of the Bambino". The Yankees, with Babe Ruth, got on an unprecedented roll. They have won 39 American League pennants and 26 world champion series titles– not all with Babe Ruth.

Meanwhile, the Boston Red Sox made it to the world champion series in 1946 and lost in game seven to the Cardinals. The Red Sox made it back to the world champion series again in 1967 and lost in game seven to the Cardinals. In 1975, the Red Sox made it back to the world champion series again and lost in game seven, to the Cincinnati Reds. The Red Sox made it back to the world champion series in 1986 and lost in game seven to the New York Mets.

Coming from New York, once I got to Boston, it was very easy to see the pattern. Boston fans are passionate about their sports. They really identify with their teams and have a very strong desire for their teams to win. The Red Sox would play great, until the All-Star break, and then the slide would start. The players would choke. Every year, the Red Sox fans would start off by saying, "This is our year!" Then, they would watch in horror as their hearts were broken once again. This went on for 86 years. Between the Red Sox players and their fans, they had a really strong desire to win but were very out of tune with winning. So, there was a lot of friction. It was very uncomfortable for the fans, players, coaches, and everyone involved. Players would come and go. Coaches would come and go. The media would tear them apart– lots of friction. The New York Yankees became the Red Sox's nemesis. The Red Sox fans hated them.

Before the 2004 season, the Red Sox had new owners, another new manager, and some high-priced players. They got new players before the Yankees could get them. Everything seemed to be in place. But was it? The end of the season came, and the Red Sox were still in the hunt to win. They still had a shot to make the playoffs and possibly the world champion series. The team was doing something right. They were more in tune with their desire. The fans were still eager and optimistic. The energy was flowing. However, most of the fans were waiting for the other shoe to drop. Sooner or later they were going to choke and start losing games. They would find a way to lose, just when it looked like they were going win. Sooner or later they would break the fans' hearts again, just like they did every year. They got all the way to the American League championship series against, you-know-who, the hated New York Yankees, and the trouble began.

Game one: the Yankees won, 10 to 7. Game two: the Yankees won, 3 to 1. Game three: the Red Sox got murdered. The Yankees scored 19 runs, and the Red Sox only scored 8. This game wasn't just a loss. It was an all-out slaughter. It seemed like every Yankee that came up to bat hit a home run.

Energetically, it was very easy for the fans to finally let go. As I watched this game, I said to Marjorie that I could feel the energy shifting. The Red Sox had done it. They had choked. They were going to lose game four and be swept. Once again, they broke their fans' hearts.

The fans, at this point, let all the friction go. It was as if they all stopped holding their breath at the same time. They finally exhaled. It was over. We are going to lose, again. They all relaxed and let it go. Oh, well. Maybe next year. That seemed to be all that was needed to finally let the energy flow. When it did finally flow, the universe delivered big-time. Imagine what 86 years of strong desire is in terms of energy. Now, it was finally free to flow.

Game four came around, and much to everyone's surprise, the Yankees didn't sweep the Red Sox. They lost. The Red Sox won, 6 to 4. Game five: the Red Sox won, 5 to 4. Game six: the Red Sox tied the series three games apiece by winning 4 to 2. Game seven: the Red Sox put away the Yankees 10 to 3. The New York papers and the media were all over the Yankees, calling the game the biggest choke in baseball history. The Yankees didn't know what hit them. But now that we understand energy flow, we know what hit them. They didn't stand a chance once the energy began to flow.

The Boston Red Sox went on to sweep the St. Louis Cardinals in four games. The Cardinals didn't know what hit them either. The Cardinals made uncharacteristic mistakes. The Red Sox finally won the world champion series.

Letting the energy flow

This story is a great illustration of becoming in tune with your desire and letting the energy flow through you. Principle three: **The universe always says yes and does not give up on you.** Everything in our universe is about the flowing of energy. Ask and you will receive, every time, without exception. We just have to get in tune with what we are asking for so that the energy flows and what we want manifests.

Let's review what we've learned so far. The entire universe is a sea of energy and vibration. This energy is for us to use and create with. We direct this energy into what we want by asking. The law of attraction is the engine that runs everything. We are asking all the time. Whenever we think about something and focus on it for 17 seconds, we are asking the universe for more of this. When we focus on something we want, we feel good. When we focus on something we don't want, since we can't say no to it, we feel bad. This is communication from our higher self, letting us know that we are trying to say no to something. We have to focus on what we want, clearly, with a single vibration. Our emotions are always letting us know if we are in or out of tune with what we want. If we are in balance with the amount of energy we are pulling through us, we feel good. If we are out of balance, we feel bad. Our beliefs act like filters. If we are asking for something and we don't believe it, we are creating friction within ourselves and our vibration. That's the process.

You now have all of your building blocks, except for one, in place. The final building block is chapter fourteen, *Self-Worth.* You now know the information for creating your life. You now have the "instruments" to start playing your own "music" of what you want. You know how to get "in tune" with your desire. The rest of the chapters are fine-tuning, just to give you a little extra balance. In the next chapter, *Imagination,* we will learn about a superpower, which helps us create. You would like to have a superpower, wouldn't you?

Summary:

Our universe is a sea of energy. We create our lives with this energy by directing it.

You create your own reality by asking and by focusing or thinking about something.

Infinite intelligence is part of the sea of energy.

The strength of your desire determines how much energy you are pulling through.

Your feelings are letting you know if you are in tune with what you asked for.

We are always asking, except when we are sleeping.

We have to be in tune with what we ask for in order for it to manifest.

The universe always says yes and does not give up on you.

Your beliefs filter your energy flow.

8

Imagination

When you were a child, did you ever wish or pretend you had superpowers? Wouldn't it be great if you could fly? Have supersonic speed, x-ray vision, or the strength of a hundred men? How about if you could be invisible? What would you say if I told you that you do have a superpower? But because of that time you burned down the school with your x-ray vision, you've been encouraged *not* to use this power that you have. While obviously I'm kidding about burning down the school, I am not kidding about you being encouraged not to use your power. But I'm getting a little ahead of myself.

You have a gift that you were born with that can help and change your life immensely. However, you've been taught to ignore it. Have you figured it out yet? Do you know what I'm talking about? You used it all the time when you were a child because it's natural to children. It's something that they all do very, very easily. This gift is your imagination, and yes, it is a superpower. You still have it, whether you use it or not. When we were kids, it was very easy for us to pretend, daydream, and imagine. We would very easily slip off into our own little worlds. By the time we started school, teachers and parents often admonished us for using it. How many times were you told to sit up and pay attention?

Visualize

It is words like pretending, daydreaming, and imagining that have the connotation of being something that children do. Let's see if we can put this into more of an adult vernacular. For example, athletes don't pretend, they visualize. A quarterback would visualize throwing the winning touchdown pass. The head of a company is not a daydreamer. He's a visionary, who visualizes his company growing and being profitable. Companies with strong goals and a good sense of focus have "vision". Artists don't daydream a picture. They see it in their mind's eye first and then create it. Actors don't pretend to be somebody else. They act. They visualize the character, with all their traits and quirks, and then inhabit the character.

Some people still visualize and use their imaginations. However, most people hardly use their imagination at all and with good reason. They were taught that it was inappropriate. *Stop daydreaming and pay attention.* It is usually something we heard from schoolteachers. We've all been in classrooms when the teachers called on the kid who was completely oblivious. The teacher calls his name a couple times. "Earth to Joey, earth to Joey. Hello! Is there anybody in there?" The kid who is daydreaming is startled back to reality, jumps, and everyone else in the classroom laughs. Joey is embarrassed and probably won't daydream in class again. He has served as an example for the rest of the kids in that class too. If you daydream in my class, you're going to be embarrassed and admonished for it. Does this sound familiar, anyone?

I would go around to different schools when I was working as a yearbook photographer. My job was taking pictures of the students. I took the candid pictures. One day, I was in a shop class photographing the kids doing their projects. I needed to get a group shot, so I rounded up the kids and got them to all stand together as a group. One of the boys in the back row was standing a bit of a distance away from the rest of the kids. I said to him, "Please move closer to this other kid. Pretend you like him for two seconds while I make this picture." His answer to my request surprised me. He said, "I don't pretend anymore. That's for children". To which I replied, "Albert Einstein didn't think so." He didn't have a response to that. He just looked at me with a blank stare. He did, however, move over so I could take the picture.

I wondered how many times he was admonished as a child for daydreaming. If there were even the slightest spark of interest, I would've happily told him about the Einstein quote and what a difference the quote made for me. "Imagination is more important than knowledge." This is my favorite quote. When I was in school, there were times when I was made to feel stupid by teachers and others. When I came across this quote, being an artist and musician, and having a very active imagination, I felt vindicated. One of the smartest men of all time said that your imagination is the most important thing. Unfortunately, the kid I was taking a picture of had already, at the age of 15, turned off his imagination.

Daydreaming

Someone who daydreamed at school a lot is Michael Flatley, who was the original lead dancer from Riverdance, and then the Lord of the Dance. He said that he spent his life daydreaming about this all the time and that teachers used to yell at him in school because he was looking out the window daydreaming about his success as a dancer. Now he's thrilled to tell people that what he used to do is daydream in school about dancing. His dreams have come true. I saw him talking about this on a television show about people who were highly successful in what they do. These people were multimillionaires. Maybe there is something to this daydreaming stuff after all. When Michael was daydreaming about dancing he wasn't trying to make it happen. He was simply enjoying his daydream. This is a very big key. When you visualize and try to make something happen, it tends to slow down the manifestation. Instead, try to just enjoy your vision.

There are lots of other famous and successful people who said they use their imagination to help them get what they want. John Lennon, one of the founding members of the most successful rock band of its time, The Beatles, even wrote a song called *Imagine.* The leaders of highly successful companies are referred to, among other things, as visionaries. For example, Bill Gates had his vision of everybody having a personal computer and using his products. Perhaps if the opportunity arises, instead of scolding a child for daydreaming, we can change the message to daydreaming is good and can help you achieve your goals. Just choose a more appropriate time to do it.

Another famous person is J. M. Barrie the author of *Peter Pan.* What do you think he was trying to tell us with Peter Pan? I believe that part of what he was trying to tell us, is that Peter Pan never wanted to grow up, because when you grow up, you stop pretending. Imagining is how your life is created. Peter Pan's belief was growing up was bad. J. M. Barrie may have also shared this belief.

In chapter six, we talked about beliefs, and we learned that if we want something that we believe we can have, we easily get it. If we want something that we have doubts about or don't really believe, then it can be a rougher ride. We learned in chapter seven, that we can ask for anything we want. If we really want something strongly enough, it doesn't matter what we believe. The strength of the desire will eventually get it to us. If we are out of tune with our desire, it will be a very uncomfortable ride, like riding in a truck with no shocks on a bumpy dirt road and having to go to the bathroom. Nice visual? Well, this is the chapter on imagining. When you want something, and you believe you can have it, you are in tune with your desire. When you want something you have doubts about, you are out of tune with your desire.

"How"

If you want something and you're out of tune with it, what do you do? You use your superpower. You imagine it. Ah, come on Ed. We imagine it? That's it? You're not going to tell me how? Not what steps I have to take, not how to break it down into small segments? Not how to set a goal? Not how to break it down into what's most important to do first and build steps from there? No, I am not going to tell you any of that. I am going to tell you how to visualize. But as far as all that other "how-to" stuff, we are not going to do any of that because right here, in the middle of my "how-to" book, I'm going to tell you that "how" is not your job. How is the universe's job. Ernest Holmes said, "We must be specific in what we do, while at the same time, never outlining how it shall be done."[25]

Remember, you direct the energy by asking and by thinking. Imagining is both asking and thinking. You recall, whatever you think about for 17 seconds, you're asking for. The law of attraction is the engine that makes it work. So, "how" is the job of the universe and the law of attraction. "How" is not your job.

The specific thing that we have to do is be similar to the vibration or frequency of our desire. That's it. The rest is up to the universe. Remember the universe always says yes and will practically stand on its head to give you what you want, which is Principle three. This is where our feelings come into play again. When I think about what I want and feel good, it's on its way. When I think about what I want, and I don't feel good, I'm out of tune with what I want, and it's not on its way.

Let's look at an example of this. When I was a kid, about seven-years-old, I decided I wanted a guitar. I was very excited about the idea of having a guitar. I was happy and my energy was flowing– I wanted a guitar. Playing this guitar was going be fun. It was going to be cool. I used to look at the guitars in the back of the Sears catalog. I still remember the one I wanted. It was green. I would look at the picture of this guitar all the time. Does that sound like visualizing to you?

Eventually, I went to an adult and said, "I want this guitar." I expected them to be just as excited about it as I was. I believe the guitar was $49. The first question this adult asked me was ***how*** I expected to pay for the guitar. I had no idea. I was just excited about the guitar and wanted it. I was told if I wanted to have the guitar, I had to figure out ***how*** to get it. I was still very excited and

25 Holmes, Ernest, *The Science of Mind A Philosophy, A Faith, A Way of Life* Jeremy P. Tarcher/Putnam 1926

had little or no concept of a job or money. To make a long story short, I ended up getting a paper route, which I absolutely hated. Dogs chased me. People didn't always pay, and it was up to the kids to go around and collect payment for the papers. Whatever money you had left after all the papers were paid for was what you made. Needless to say, I did not make that much. I still, to this day, remember the giant St. Bernard who used to chase me. I swear the people put the dog outside on the day that I was supposed to collect the money.

Anyway, I never got the guitar from Sears. However, I did get a guitar. A friend of mine, who was in a band (that was the next thing I wanted– to be in a band) sold me his first guitar and amp for $20. Even though I became out of tune with my desire once someone asked me ***"how"*** I was going to get the guitar, I still had a strong enough desire to get a guitar. It wasn't the exact one I thought I wanted, but it was a guitar. Yes, I quit the paper route. But from then on, I always thought that ***"how"*** was my job. ***"How"*** is the universe's job. Your job is to be in tune with your desire.

Visualizing

A good way to get in tune with your desire is by imagining or visualizing. You can also change your beliefs, which we've already talked about. If what you want is really important to you, I recommend you do both, visualize and change your beliefs. There are probably lots of ways to imagine and visualize. I'm going to tell you two ways. But before we get to that, let's take a look at some people who use their imagination and visualize in their everyday lives. If you watch Olympic athletes before their events, you can usually see them going over their performance in their heads. Some of them have their eyes closed and are making small movements with their bodies. Some are just standing perfectly still, sort of staring off into space. Which method they are using does not matter. All that matters is that they are using their imagination and getting in tune with their desire. The clearer that they can imagine their performance, the more in tune with it they are.

Lawrence Taylor, probably the greatest linebacker to ever play football, said that when he was a kid playing in his backyard, he would always imagine himself making the big plays, and he would do a running commentary in his head. *Lawrence Taylor breaks through the line rounding the corner. They try to block him, but they can't. Knocking the football out of the quarterback's hands, he scoops up the ball and runs for a touchdown. The fans go wild.* For those of you who aren't familiar with football, the fans went wild for Lawrence Taylor every single game he played. He was truly a football superstar. If you could speak to the superstars of every sport, you would find out that almost all the players imagine or visualize and that the superstars are very good at it.

Actors also have very good and active imaginations. They have to take the words that someone else wrote and make them into a living, breathing, and believable character. The better that they can get themselves out of the way and fully imagine or pretend that they are this person, the better their performance will be. The actors in a movie like *Star Wars* had to use their imagination because the movie used a special effect called the "blue screen", where there is no background, foreground, nothing. It's all put in afterwards, as the shot is put together. So, in the fight scenes where they're jumping from level to level with all the robots and the alien creatures, most of that stuff wasn't even there. Imagine how good you have to be at imagining when you have to act a movie scene when there's nothing there but blue, and you have to talk to other characters like they're there, when they are not. Did you see Jennifer Connelly in *The Hulk*? She was basically talking to nothing, because the Hulk character was computer-generated afterwards.

Writers use their imaginations to create stories out of thin air. I assure you, the worlds that they created were very much alive and well in their minds. How else would they so clearly be able to describe it to you, so that you could also see it in your imagination, or "mind's eye", if you prefer. J.M. Barrie could certainly see Neverland, the pirate ship, Captain Hook, Smee, Wendy and her brothers, and, of course, Peter Pan. He could see them in his mind as clearly as you and I see "reality".

Musicians also can usually hear the music and the words to the songs in their heads when they get into the creative zone to write. Mozart heard all the music he wrote in his head. He could hear it so clearly that all he needed to do was write it down. Beethoven became deaf towards the end of his life but could still hear the music inside his head. Visual artists like photographers and painters see the work in their mind's eye before they create it in this physical reality. Visual artists look for things that catch their attention. For a landscape painter, it might be the sunlight glistening off a beautiful lake with the mountains in the background. From seeing that scene, the painter would get a vision in his mind's eye of what a painting of that scene would look like and then paint the scene.

Do you see how important your imagination is? You don't have to be an artist or an athlete to use your imagination. I know plenty of salespeople who imagine their sales before they call on the customers. Now, contrary to popular belief, that does not give them some kind of super selling power, where they can sell things to people who don't want them. What it does do is get them in tune with their desire of making a sale, and the law of attraction brings them customers who want to buy what they're selling.

Reactivate your imagination

Let's have some fun. Let's reactivate your imagination. Just relax. We will do it together. I'll walk you through it. It's going to be fun and easy.

Do you remember when you were a kid, how easy it was to pretend? Well, let me refresh your memory. Do you remember playing in the big box that your parents got from a refrigerator or washer or dryer? What was it? Was it a dollhouse? Was it a cave or a fort or a rocket ship or a racing car? You had a great imagination as a kid, and it's still there. It might be asleep, but it's still there. When you were a child, a stick could be any one of a million things. I was talking to a friend of mine the other day, and he told me his son's favorite toys right now are an old shoe box and a white towel. He puts one on his head and runs around with the towel playing with them. Only he knows for sure what they're supposed to be.

We all have this capacity to imagine, pretend, and daydream. Or, if you prefer the grown-up word, visualize. We never lose it. It might not be active in you right now, but you still have it. Our imagination is that natural to all of us.

Let's do some fantasizing or visualizing. The easiest way to get back into this is to ask questions. As you read these questions try to take a couple of seconds and let mental images start forming in your mind's eye. If you don't know the answer to some of these questions, don't worry about it. It's not a test. Just go on to the next one.

What kind of life do you want?

What do you want to do?

What is fun to you?

Where do you want to live?

What does the house you want to live in look like?

What color is it?

Is it in an urban setting, or is it in the country?

Does it have lots of land?

Is it near or on the water?

Are there gardens?

Does it have a swimming pool?

Is there a deck or a patio?

Would the pool be more of a natural setting?

Maybe with a waterfall?

Can you imagine yourself sitting out there in a lounge chair, feeling the warmth of the sun on your body while you're relaxing?

What does the inside of the house look like?

What would you love to have in your house?

Are there paintings on the walls?

Do you have photographs on the walls of your family?

Can you see them in your mind's eye?

How big is the kitchen?

Does it smell like someone's been baking?

Maybe cookies or cinnamon rolls or a nice, warm, fresh-out-of-the oven apple pie?

Can you smell it?

What else is in the kitchen?

Granite countertops?

What do the cabinets look like?

How about the appliances?

Is there plenty of room to work, lots of countertops?

Is there an island?

How about a built-in wine cooler?

How many burners on the cook top?

Do you have a single or double oven?

Does it have a regular fridge or a fridge with paneling on the front to match your cabinets?

Are you getting the idea? Is it starting to come back to you? How easily can you picture this in your mind's eye? With a little practice you will be able to easily do this whenever you want. The law of attraction will make it easier for you, every time you do it. This is fun, isn't it? Let's keep going. Let's try another subject. How about an outdoor activity? Maybe something like golf.

Do you play golf?

What would the perfect day of golf feel like?

Would you start out early in the morning or a little bit later in the day?

Would you play by yourself, with someone else, or make a foursome?

What would the weather be like?

A nice sunny day, a little bit cool with a bit of a breeze, but not too much wind to blow your ball off-course?

Where are you playing? Pebble Beach? Bermuda? Hawaii? Florida? St. Andrews in Scotland?

Where is your favorite golf course?

Or better yet, where is the course that you would love to play on?

Did you pick a favorite golf course? Good, let's play a round there.

How does your body feel?

Are you loose and relaxed?

How is your swing on this fine day?

How are you hitting the ball?

How about when you're putting, are you in the zone?

How are the greens?

Are they fast or slow?

Has the grass been cut recently, and can you smell it in the air?

You're remembering how to visualize and imagine, aren't you? You remember how much fun it was to imagine and pretend when you were a kid? It's coming back. It's still alive within you. You just have to practice it and do it often. Why? Because it feels good. You remember what feeling good means. But just in case you forgot, when you feel good, everything that you want is easily flowing to you.

Visualization, "A walk on the beach"

Let's do one together. How about we go for a walk on the beach, no not in Maine. How about in Florida? How about the west coast of Florida on Sanibel Island where the beaches have lots of shells? It's early in the morning. It's late spring, around the end of April. The sun is just coming up. The air feels a little bit humid this morning. There's a slight breeze. The sun is rising, and as you look around, you can see it has put a natural golden glow on everything. As you walk across the boardwalk to the beach, hear the gentle sound of your sneakers against the boards. You feel the boards give a little bit underneath your feet as you step on them. At the end of the boardwalk, you step down into the sand, which makes a whooshing sound as your feet sink into the loose sand, which is surprisingly cooler than you expected. As you stop and look over the beach, you see there are shells everywhere, and you decide to keep your sneakers on. You're comfortably dressed. You have your favorite "I'm on vacation" shirt on and a comfortable pair of jeans. It's probably about 72° outside. It's a beautiful sunny morning.

There are a few puffy clouds in the sky that are golden yellow, and the sky is a beautiful shade of blue. As you stand there and look up and down the beach, you see a couple of people out walking along. There's a man who jogs by. There are a few people who are obviously collecting shells. They keep bending over every couple of steps. Over all, it is pretty quiet. You decide to walk up the beach, with the wind at your back. You start walking. You angle over towards where the surf flattens out the sand. Once you get there, the packed sand is easier to walk on. As you walk on the beach, every few steps crunch, sounding like eating a bowl of crispy cereal. You never realized how many shells were on the beach, and you think to yourself, it's a good thing I have my sneakers on. The sun is glistening off the water making beautiful, golden diamonds of light that seem to be dancing on the surface.

Occasionally, you hear the sound of a sea gull calling as it flies by. As you walk, you hear a little bit of a commotion off to the side. As you stop to look, you see a whole bunch of pelicans up in the trees starting to flap their wings making some funny noises. They appear to be talking to each other. You think to yourself, so that's where pelicans go at night, up in the trees. You take a deep breath and smell the fresh ocean air. You slowly inhale as you enjoy the scent of it. You start walking again. You can hear the surf gently rolling the shells. You're surprised at how many there are. It sounds like pouring uncooked pasta shells out of the box, which makes you smile when you think about the sound. You are enjoying your walk. Your body feels good. You feel relaxed, open, free, really enjoying this peaceful morning walk.

You hear sound out in the water and turn just in time to see a dolphin's dorsal fin about 30 feet off shore, slowly swimming by. Looking over the water, you see two more pop out behind the first one. They seem to be just slowly rolling along, sliding out and rolling back into the water and rolling up again and back into the water. It's almost as if they're dancing or flying. This glorious sense of peace comes over you as you watch them swimming by. You turn and continue to walk. Your eye catches something unusual in the sand. Something green. Bending over, you look at it. It's a beautiful piece of dark green sea glass, a very rare treasure indeed. Picking it up to take a closer look, it glistens in your hand. It's been in the ocean for a while, and it's perfectly rounded, about the size of a dime. Putting it in your pocket, you smile. What fun it is to find treasure. Continuing to walk, you realize you don't have your watch with you, and it brings another smile to your face. You say to yourself, this is a glorious morning, and I'm just going to continue walking.

Can you feel it? Are you there on the beach having a walk? Can you hear the sounds of the ocean? Can you smell the ocean air? Are the shells crunching under your feet as you walk? That's all you need to do– imagine, pretend. Okay, I'll use the adult word, visualize. It was easy, wasn't it? As I mentioned earlier, the more you do it the easier it gets. Your imagination is still alive and well. This visualizing stuff isn't so hard after all. Pablo Picasso once said, "Everything you can imagine is real." Start imagining.

To get in tune with what you're asking for, you have to believe that you can have what you want. Visualizing or imagining is another way for you to change your beliefs. Because when you're enjoying your vision, the universe can't tell the difference between what you're imagining and the "real world." You recall that your vibration, the song that you are playing inside of yourself, comes from whatever you're focusing on. The law of attraction simply matches vibrations. That's all it does. There is no thought or judgment about the content of the vibration. The law of attraction is always consistent and simply does its job, which is to match the vibration. The song that you are playing can be the real world right now or a memory from the past or a visualization of the future. The universe can't tell the difference. The law of attraction starts to give you whatever you pay attention to (think about) for approximately 17 seconds.

Many ways to visualize

There are many ways to visualize. I'm going to tell you about two that will help you get what you want. The first is to visualize what you actually want. Think about your desire, what you're asking for, and imagine that you have it. Do it just the way we did earlier– ask questions. *What would it be like if I was doing ________? Where am I? What am I doing? How do I feel?* Just make up a story about you doing, or having, whatever it is you're asking for. Try to get as many senses involved as possible. What does it feel like? What does it smell like? What does it taste like? Continue on from there. Now, remember the most important thing is how you feel. If you think about your desire, and you don't feel good, you're not getting it. Right? You remember, when you're feeling good, everything you want is easily flowing to you. When you're not, it's not flowing.

The second way is what I call taking a vacation in your mind. The goal again is to feel good. All you do is what we did earlier in this chapter when we talked about the house, walking on the beach, playing golf. If you have a favorite vacation spot or a favorite day off, go back and revisit those things often. If not, make up a new one. You're completely unlimited. This is your vacation, and you can go anywhere in the world. You have all the time and all the money and whatever else you need to do anything you want. Make it as enjoyable as possible. Where would you go? What time of year would it be? Do you go by yourself or do you bring someone with you? What would you do? You're completely unlimited. You can do anything from horseback riding to skydiving to fishing to painting to making love to going to a restaurant and having a great meal or to doing absolutely nothing and taking a nap. This is your visualization. There are no rules and no limits. Just ask yourself questions. The goal is to feel as good as you can.

Key component

A couple of other points about imagining and visualizing –the purpose of this is fun. This is not supposed to be work. You're supposed to enjoy it. You want to keep an easy, loose, and relaxed feeling to this, sort of gently enjoying, rather than trying too hard to will something into being. Did you ever try to will yourself to sleep? The harder you tried, the more awake you became? I'll tell you how to easily fall asleep in chapter sixteen, *Exercises.* You want to feel playful, relaxed, and comfortable. Avoid anything that causes anxiety or nervousness. Just relax and have fun. Be a kid again and play. When you were a kid in your daydream, you were not trying to create something. You were just having fun in your daydream. Keep this in mind when you're imagining and visualizing. It is a key component to all of this. With a little practice, you will find that you can imagine any time you want.

Is there a best time to imagine or visualize? The short answer is no. However, one of the best times to visualize is when you first wake up in the morning because you can easily connect with your higher self. You're still in that energy. When we talk about meditating in chapter sixteen, one of the best times to meditate is also right when you wake up in the morning before you get your day started. So, what I usually do is meditate and then visualize. Another good time is when you're in the shower because no one can get to you and bother you, no telephones, no interruptions.

Right before you go to sleep at night is also a good time to imagine. You'll have to find a balance in this because if you get too excited, you won't be able to sleep. It's a good time to gently, easily imagine what you want. If your imagination is about being somewhere in a comfortable chair by the pool or in the mountains or wherever, and quietly taking a nap, that's a great visualization to help you get to sleep. Doing your visualization just before you go to sleep will also put it into your subconscious. When you wake up in the morning, you will be in the same frequency, and you may dream about it and stay in that frequency most of the night. I try to do it a few times a day, whenever I can steal a minute or two, here and there. Think of it as just taking a two-minute vacation, a couple of times a day. The more you visualize, the easier it will be to do. The more you visualize, the more you will believe your desire and become the same frequency as it and the sooner you will receive it. Both visualizations work equally as well. Remember the goal is to feel good.

I hope you enjoyed this chapter as much as I did. I hope we've awakened your imagination, and the kid inside of you is ready to play again. As we conclude this chapter, there is no better time than now to start using your imagination. Since we have our building blocks in place, we are going to continue with the fine-tuning. Your imagination is a very powerful tool. It's your superpower to help you with your fine- tuning. When is the best time to use your superpower? The answer to that is the subject of our next chapter.

Summary:

Your imagination is alive and well. It is your "superpower".

"Imagination is more important than knowledge." Albert Einstein

Your imagination is one of the most powerful tools you have to create your life.

"Reality" is not as real as you think, and it's easy to change.

The inner world of our mind is where our world is created.

Use your imagination to bring yourself in tune with your desire.

"How" is not your job. The universe takes care of the "how's".

Athletes who visualize their performance are more in tune with their desires. You can do this also.

Imagination is natural and innate to everyone. You just have to wake it back up by using it.

Ask yourself questions to get into your visualizations or fantasies.

Take a "vacation in your mind." No limits at all. Just feel good.

The purpose is to have fun. Enjoy and feel good.

Remember when you were a kid who was daydreaming. You were enjoying your daydream, not trying to make something happen.

Enjoy your vision without trying too hard to make it happen.

9

Now

Now is all there is. You can't go back to the past and change it. Done is done. You can't jump into the future and live then because if you could, then that would become now. Now, is now, whether you're in Boston, Hawaii, China, India, Paris, Los Angeles, Tennessee, Texas, or New York. No matter where you are in the world, right now is now. The moment "now" is the same everywhere.

The past

As we begin to talk about now, we need to first talk about the past. In our memories, we can go back and relive the past. Depending on how focused you are, you can relive your past experiences to whatever extent you want. Now that you know how powerful your imagination is, you will see how powerful reviewing past events in your memory can be. Whatever you think about clearly for 17 seconds, you start to vibrate, and the law of attraction begins to match it. You can relive past events, emotionally and "vibrationally", as much as you want. You can just lightly recall the memory, or you can jump back in, and depending on how strong the emotions of the event were, you can reactivate that vibration or frequency of the memory, play the song from back then, within you, and essentially bring the vibration of the past event to your right now. If the memory was something that you enjoyed or in some way thrilled you or was one of the happiest days of your life, then doing this would be fun and you would feel good. You all know by now that feeling good is the key. Because when we feel good, everything we want flows easily to us.

However, if by reviewing the past, in your memory or your mind's eye, you beat yourself up for things you did or for the way things worked out, then this is an exercise in futility. For two reasons: First, bringing up negative memories from the past doesn't feel good, and you all know what that means, right? You have brought the song that you were playing in the past into your "right now". As you focus on this song, you are playing it to the universe. That becomes your vibration right now. You know that whatever song you're playing in your "right now" is what you're telling the universe you want. So, let me ask you, do you want more of those negative experiences from the past? I didn't think so.

The second reason you don't want to beat yourself up about what happened in the past is that there is nothing you can do about it. The past is over. It's done. You can't physically get yourself back into the past and make the past your "right now", so there's nothing you can do about it. There is no way you can change it. Yes, I hear you, but if I focus on the past event and examine it, I can learn from my mistakes in the past. Can you? Sometimes we use the past as evidence of what is possible instead of using our thoughts to create what we want and desire. Anything is possible. If you can imagine it, then you can live it. The past does not equal the future. In your "right now" you have complete and total free will. You always have a choice. You can choose that things are getting better or that things are getting worse, but either way, you always have a choice.

Focusing on the past with the idea of learning from your mistakes so you don't re-create what you did in the past, only works when you identify the mistake, and then visualize it done correctly in the future. However, as soon as you start doing this, you are no longer reliving the past. You are now imagining your future, which is something I recommend. To illustrate this, let's say you went on a job interview, and you were very nervous, unprepared, and did a lousy job. You decide that you want to do better on the next interview. So, you imagine it. You see yourself feeling confident and sure. You see yourself arriving early. You imagine reaching into your pocket and pulling out your list of questions that you have for the person who is interviewing you. This time, it's a double interview. Not only are they interviewing you, but also you are interviewing them. Your vision will continue from there, depending on what you imagine, and how you want it to go. Before we talk about now, let's take a quick visit to the future.

The future

Let's talk about the future. Well, the future never gets here, because as soon as the future gets here, it's now, and it's no longer the future. However, what we can do is create our future in our now. We are doing this whether we know it or not. Principle five: **You create your own reality, even if you don't know you're doing it.** We can do it on purpose or we can do it by accident. I'm guessing because you made it this far into the book that you want to do this on purpose. Remember, earlier I said we are "asking machines". We are always playing a song within us, and we are always sending off a vibration, except when we are sleeping. If you are imagining and meditating and paying attention to how you feel and using your affirmations, then you are creating your future on purpose. You are doing it by choice. If you are just going along and letting the turbulence and drama of life control how you feel, then you are creating by accident or letting "reality" and your re-actions to it, create your life. Either way is fine. Remember, you always have a choice. I suggest you choose the first way. The only time you are creating, either on purpose or by accident, is now.

Now is where all the creation takes place. Now is where the universe, hearing the song that you're playing, starts playing it along with you. The law of attraction is working right now. The song you are playing inside of you is what you are directing the sea of energy to do. Creation is taking place by what you think, and all of your thinking is done in the now. That is why **now is so important.**

Mindful vs Mindless

I also want to talk about the Zen philosophy of now, which is to be mindful and fully conscious in the moment, which is your now. You have a choice to be mindful or mindless in every moment. Let's start by looking at examples of things that people do mindlessly. A lot of people mindlessly watch TV. When you're watching TV you become the vibration or frequency of that show. The last thing you watch at night before you go to bed, is the song or vibration that you are taking to bed with you. If you mindlessly watch TV, because it's a habit or because you're supposed to watch the news, that's what you're taking to bed with you every night. Is watching a mostly negative newscast the song or vibration you want to be playing when you go to bed at night? I have said that you are not vibrating or creating when you're sleeping. The reason you don't want to take a negative vibration with you to bed is because your mood can affect how well you sleep. When you wake up in the morning, you wake back up into the vibration you were in when you went to sleep. If you go to sleep in a bad mood, you usually will wake up in a bad mood. Taking a negative vibration to bed with you probably isn't a good idea. Don't you agree?

People also tend to mindlessly drive. Have you ever driven past your exit and not realized it til you went by? Have you ever, all of a sudden, realized you have no idea where you are? We are creatures of habit. We have something that's referred to as muscle memory, which simply means we learned something and turned it over to our subconscious. Now we do it without even thinking about it. We say something has become ingrained in us. That's the way most of us drive. I'm not specifically talking about the knowing how to drive. I'm talking about not paying attention as we are driving. Being fully mindful and fully conscious and in the moment is a much safer way to drive. It's your life, you get to choose to be fully conscious or not.

Mindful practice

Guitar playing and performing are very similar to exercising and working out. I'm sure that some of you who work out know exactly what I mean about your mind wandering. When you're working out, once you know the routine, it can be like practicing a musical instrument. It becomes ingrained and a habit. But staying fully conscious while you're doing your exercises can make a big difference. What you need to do with anything like working out or practicing an instrument is to try to vary as much as possible whenever you can. If every Monday you work on your upper body or that's when you play all your major scales, then within as little as four weeks, you will get bored. When you're bored, your mind easily just wanders. When your mind wanders, you lose focus. If you do something without focus, you are not really gaining any benefit, whether playing a musical instrument or working out or any other form of repetitive practice. The idea is to make it enough of a habit so that you keep doing it but not so much of a habit that it gets boring. I know. Easier said than done. Abraham-Hicks suggested to me that I practice in my mind. Use your imagination to see yourself "practicing" in your mind. This increases your focus and concentration, and it helps you be fully conscious when you practice. This also gets the law of attraction involved because doing it in your mind is thinking about it. Thinking, as we all know by now, is how we get what we want. When you practice in your mind, you still exercise your muscles but without the full strain of your whole practice routine. Try it. This will work on many things, from playing a musical instrument to playing a sport to drawing or painting or other forms of artistic expression. This will work with virtually anything. Practicing in your mind will help increase your focus and help you stay in the now. It will also be easier when you're actually practicing and/or doing your chosen activity.

Mindful of how you feel

Another thing that people tend to mindlessly do is not pay attention to how they're feeling. We've talked about feelings many times. You know that's how you navigate through your life. Also, your feelings are your indicator of how you're doing. We've all seen people have some drama in their day and then continue to be in that same mood for the rest of the day, sometimes even longer. You always have a choice. We've talked about this earlier. Do you want to be right or do you want to feel good? You know by now that feeling good is the "right" answer.

The point is to choose when to be fully conscious in the moment or when not to be fully conscious. I don't know if it's possible to be fully conscious every waking moment of every day. But if that's your goal or desire, I hope you can do it. What I would like to convey to you is that you do have a choice to be fully conscious or not. **Be fully conscious when you're creating your life**, whether you're imagining, meditating, doing your affirmations, or doing some of the other exercises that we will talk about in chapter sixteen.

Being fully conscious can also help you when you're nervous or anxious. For example, I remember watching the *Oprah Winfrey Show* after the Academy Awards one year, and Oprah was talking to Hilary Swank, who had just won the Oscar the night before. Hilary talked about being nervous and anxious. She said that what she did was really focus on staying in the moment, being fully conscious. She really paid attention to every category, as they came up, and listened to what the people had to say when they won– their speeches, their thank-yous, their gratitude for winning, etc. She said she was so good at staying in the moment that she was quite surprised when it was her turn for the award and equally surprised when she won. She explained that she really didn't have a chance to get nervous, and she was able to stay in the moment. Being fully conscious and staying in the moment is the same thing. Your decision to be fully in the now, fully conscious and focused, also means a decision to be fully alive.

Right now is where everything takes place. Right now, you are playing your song, which is more like a symphony being played by a gigantic orchestra. The universe is joining in and playing your song with you and giving you what you're asking for and that's all happening right now in this instant, and every instant that you're awake. Also, right now, you are deciding to be fully conscious or scattered all over the place or completely mindless. Again, this is all happening right now. Is now important? The answer is, obviously, yes. The importance of now, its significance in your life, is up to you in every moment.

As we wrap up this chapter, we continue with our fine-tuning. We help tune ourselves by being fully focused in the now. We have our feelings guiding us, and the opportunity, in every moment, to be fully conscious. When we are doing this, and choosing our thoughts, we are certainly creating our own reality and doing it on purpose. In the next chapter we are going to continue our fine-tuning. We will take another look at the emotional scale (from chapter two). You will get a clear understanding of it and also learn how to move up the scale towards feeling good.

Summary

All of your power is right now.

You are asking the universe for what you want in every moment that you are awake.

The past is over. You cannot go back and fix it. Let it go.

You can use your imagination to build your future.

You decide to be fully conscious or mindless or somewhere in between.

When you choose to be mindless, you are no longer choosing what song you play to the world and to the universe.

10

Giant Steps

Giant Step is a song written by legendary jazz saxophone player John Coltrane. It's a song that's played fast and has "giant steps" between the chord changes. If we take a look at the C major scale, the notes are: C D E F G A B C. If we play chords or melody notes that are next to each other like, C to D, that's considered a step. If we play chords or melody notes that are further apart, like, C to G, that's considered a big jump or a giant step. You will see the relevance of this as you read further, and, no, you won't need to understand music theory to understand this chapter.

Let's start by defining what a giant step is: A giant step is trying to make a big jump from here to *over there*, while skipping the journey that it takes to get over there. A giant step is like instant gratification. For example, today is the last day of work before you go on vacation. You have a lot of work to do today, a lot of loose ends to tie up, and things to finish up before you go. Wouldn't it be nice if you could just snap your fingers and all the work was done, and you could go on vacation now? The biggest example of this is winning the lottery. If I could just somehow win this money, then my life would be great, and I would be happy. A giant step is some sort of magical quick-fix.

Instant gratification

We live in an instant gratification society, where the bottom line is what is considered to be most important. We are so completely focused on the end results, that the ends justify the means. We've completely forgotten that life is a journey, an adventure. We have forgotten Principle ten: **Life is meant to be fun**. We are told things like: *Life is short so make the best of it. You only get one chance. This is my one shot. Time is of the essence. Failure is not an option.* We also develop expectations based on our age. By the time I'm 21, I want to have accomplished this and this. By the time I'm 30, I'll be.... and by the time I'm 40, I'll be...

How many of us are living our lives like that? For parents with little children, how long does it take, when you get into the car, before you hear a chorus of "Are we there yet? Are we there yet? Are we there yet?" How did we get to this? How did we forget that life is supposed to be fun and an adventure? Why are we so obsessed with getting it done? We've all heard the expression *stop and smell the roses.* Do any of us do it?

Why don't we stop and smell the roses? We don't for a couple reasons. Some of us have learned that you have to do all your work before you can do the fun stuff. When everything is checked off my to-do list, then I can relax and have fun. You can play once your homework is done. You can't have any dessert until you eat everything that's on your plate. This leaves us always in a big hurry to "get it done", because the fun starts when it's done. The second reason we are in a hurry is we believe that the doing of the task/job is going to be hard, difficult, tedious, boring, cumbersome, exhausting or maybe even painful.

No magic pill

Let's look at some examples of giant steps from real life. There are a lot of people concerned about how much they weigh. They want to be thin or thinner. Now this is where the giant step comes in. They are looking for some magical way to quickly get them *over there. Over there,* in this case, is being the body shape and size that they want. They're looking for a magic bullet or an overnight cure because they believe that going on a diet or changing their lifestyle will be a struggle and/or uncomfortable. They've created beliefs about dieting, food, and exercising. They may also have a distorted image of what their body looks like or should look like. Since they don't know what you now know from reading this book, they are not looking for a way to change their beliefs. They don't know how to use their thoughts, imagination, and the law of attraction to create what they want. They are simply looking for a giant step. If they could magically giant step to *over there* and skip the journey, they would feel better.

Here's another example from the sports world. Jumping from being a rookie right into being a superstar is a giant step. Pittsburgh Steelers quarterback Ben Roethlisberger seems to fit the description of an overnight sensation. It appears, on the surface, that he made the giant step from being a rookie to being a superstar. He was the 2004 offensive rookie of the year. He's the first quarterback to go 13 and 0 in a season, rookie or otherwise. He appeared to have come out of nowhere and become a superstar. But if we look a little more closely, he has been playing football since he was a kid. He was an All-American in college. He was also slightly older than most rookie quarterbacks. Although what he did in his rookie season was spectacular, it was hardly a giant step for him. It just appeared to be a giant step to the rest of us because we had never heard of him or knew of his background. His football journey began years before.

Do,do,do

Football and other sports are associated with hard work, struggle, and a lot of doing. Our society glorifies struggle, martyrdom, and hard work as a means to justify the end results. Society also glorifies fame and celebrity. Yet, we end up getting contradictory signals. We are told that hard work, struggle, and sacrifice are the way to get what we want. Then we see the latest trend of being famous and successful for doing little or nothing. Innately, we know that struggle is not the way and that's why we avoid it.

If struggle were something good, it would feel good. People, in general, don't know about flowing energy, the law attraction, or how to get what they want. Instead of using thoughts and energy, we've been taught to use action. Do, do, do. Our thoughts and our beliefs create our world, and no matter how hard you work or how hard you try to "do", no amount of "doing" will change that fact.

Do you remember Principle ten: **Life is meant to be fun?** So, let me ask you. Are you having fun? Are you enjoying the moment? Are you enjoying the journey? Or are you so focused on getting it done, getting *over there,* that you're not enjoying the here and now? We know the importance of now. Have you heard the expression *human being rather than a human doing*? Which are you?

Do it in your mind

If there is something in your life that you would like to take a giant step over, the only way to do it is in your mind. We've talked about the power of thoughts, beliefs, and your imagination. If you want to get from *here* to *over there*, you need to use your imagination. You need to see yourself, in your mind, being, doing, or having what you want. See yourself enjoying the journey. See yourself all the way *over there,* where you want to be. You have to play the song of *over there* more then you're playing the song of *right now.* The goal is to enjoy the daydream of being *over there,* rather than trying to make it happen. When you are feeling good and flowing your energy, you will know what action to take. You will be inspired from within. Remember feeling good is communication from your higher self to your conscious self. Your higher self knows what you want and how to guide you to it. Earlier we talked about Michael Flatley daydreaming about dancing. He wasn't trying to be a dancer or make it happen. He was just enjoying his vision. This is an important key.

Amnesia

Let's take a look at a favorite soap opera plot. Our character somehow ends up with amnesia. She doesn't remember who she is, where she comes from, or what she does for a living. If you were able to take a giant step and completely change your life, you'd probably freak out. It would be like waking up with amnesia. Where am I? How did I get here?

What do I do next? Your world would be topsy-turvy, and you would definitely experience some major growing pains. If, somehow, today, you got what you've been wanting to giant step over, would you be ready for it? Or, would it be like waking up with amnesia? Have you thought about what it would be like to giant step? Have you imagined it? Do you enjoy going into your vision of it? What song are you playing? Is it the song of your vision or the song of where you are now? If you want it so bad that it hurts, or it's uncomfortable, then you're nowhere near having it. Remember what our feelings are telling us. You want to imagine this in your mind and feel good while you're thinking about it. If you are, then you're taking steps to it, and, sooner or later, you will have it. If you use your thoughts, it will not be a giant step. You won't wake up one day with "amnesia" and freak out, because you've been thinking and enjoying the vision of what you want and will be ready for it when it manifests.

The emotional scale

We've been talking about giant steps in reference to jumping over things in the physical world. Now, we are going to take a look at giant steps as it refers to our beliefs. Do you remember the emotional scale from chapter two? Every subject has an emotional scale within you. Money, love, children, dogs, drawing, work, school, food, exercise, geometry, sex, learning a foreign language, are some examples of subjects. Every single subject has an emotional scale. For every single subject within you, you have a belief about it. Your belief acts like a filter and filters how much energy you allow to flow about that subject, which controls how you feel about that subject. This is why I referred to you as a gigantic orchestra, rather than just one musical instrument. Think about the millions of subjects in the world. Now you see what I mean by a gigantic orchestra.

Now for the good news. Not every single subject is playing at the same time. Only some of them are playing. The ones that are playing are awake. Or, as I call them "awake vibrations" or frequencies. Each one of these has its own emotional scale set to whatever frequency it might be. If we took all of the subjects within you that are awake, at any given time, and averaged all of the different vibrations together, the average would equal your overall feeling or mood. It's the average of these that is the song that you're playing right now. When you feel bad, the average of all your awake vibrations are all on the lower end of the emotional scales of each subject. When you feel good, the average of all your awake vibrations are all on the higher end of all the emotional scales of each subject. Let's take a look at the emotional scale again.

10 love
9 joy
8 appreciation
7 passion
6 enthusiasm
5 happiness
4 belief
3 trust
2 optimism
1 hope
0 contentment
-1 boredom
-2 pessimism
-3 frustration
-4 worry
-5 blame
-6 discouragement
-7 anger
-8 revenge

-9 hate
-10 guilt
-11 grief
-12 depression

Every subject that's awake in you is playing somewhere on that scale. The ones that keep coming up and getting in your way are your beliefs that are low on the scale. Let's take a look at another way to change beliefs.

Moving up the emotional scale

Let's try this and see how it works. Let's say that the belief that keeps coming up, that seems to be holding you back, is I can't draw as well as I want to.

What are we going to do? We're going to think. Keep in mind that we want to move up the emotional scale. Let's say that we are at about minus three, frustration. We are just a little way down into the negative. We start thinking thoughts about drawing. What we are looking for are thoughts that feel good. Sound familiar? When you hit upon a thought that moves you up, you will feel it resonate within you. You will feel it harmonize with you and feel that energy surge like you feel in an "aha" moment. Now as we start, the energy is going to be small, so you have to pay attention to notice how it feels. As we get rolling, it will be easier and easier to feel which ones feel better.

Let's give it a try. *My drawing doesn't look like what I want it to.* That thought doesn't feel good. It is going in the wrong direction. Let's try again. *I do enjoy the time I spend drawing. I must have some skill and talent because my drawing looks somewhat like what I was drawing.* Those two were good. Let's keep going. *There's usually some part in my drawing that I think is good. It's silly to think that doing a little drawing every week would make me as good as one of my favorite artists. I can see for the amount of time that I get to draw that I can draw pretty well. I can see that beating myself up, by comparing my work to someone else's, is not really helpful at all. If I could spend all my time drawing, I might be as good as (insert your favorite artist here). I really do enjoy drawing, and I've decided to stop comparing my work to that of others.* Now does that sound like we've reached hope or optimism? It does to me. Now we are about six steps up the scale from where we started. No giant steps, just easily moving up the scale step-by-step, skipping a few here and there when it's not a big stretch for us to do so. That's how you do it. You look for thoughts that feel good. Just like we did when we were doing the affirmations.

Did you ever see a cartoon where someone has an idea, and a light bulb is drawn over his head? That's a good image to keep in mind. When you come up with a bright idea, you're letting your energy flow. You're feeling the energy surge. You're having an "aha" moment. That's why you light up when your energy is flowing. Remember from back in chapter four, that we are consciousness, energy, and electricity. The person who originally came up with this cartoon innately knew that energy flowing is like electricity. In the beginning, as you start to do this, the feeling is subtle, and as you gain momentum, it gets stronger and stronger. You have to pay attention to how you're feeling, which I know you can do.

The question is this: Are you going to keep playing the same song inside of you so that your world does not change, and the things you want to manifest in your life don't seem to come? Or, are you going to start playing the song of something else in your imagination and move up the emotional scale when necessary so that the things that you want start manifesting in your life? It's up to you.

Review

As we wrap up this chapter and continue with our fine-tuning, let's review: The universe is a vast sea of energy for us to use to create with. We direct this energy with our thoughts. When we think about something for 17 seconds, the law of attraction begins to match it, which starts to direct the energy towards what we want to create. Asking, desiring, and imagining are all forms of thought, and they direct the energy. The only time we can direct the energy is right now. What we believe are also thoughts, which are the foundation of what we live. Our beliefs act as filters and control how much of the energy we allow to flow. Our feelings are communication from our higher self to our conscious self. When we feel good, our energy is flowing. When we feel bad, our energy is not. Our feelings are always with us, 24/7, so we always know, in every moment, how we're doing, as long as we check how we feel. The song that we are sending off to the universe is the average vibration of every subject that is currently awake within us. We can change our vibration anytime we want by simply changing the thoughts that we are thinking and noticing how that change feels. Our thoughts are much more powerful than action. When we are feeling good and in the flow, we will be inspired as to what action to take. Trying to take a giant step over something is not the best choice. We can use our imagination to enjoy our journey and the accomplishment of our goal.

That pretty much catches us up to where we are. Now the only thing we need to do is decide what we want. Our world is set up in a way to help us decide. The next chapter is about the events that help us decide. You do know what you want, don't you?

Summary:

Principle ten: **Life is meant to be fun.**

Stop and smell the roses every now and then.

Giant steps are not the most comfortable or the best solution.

If you want to get from *here* to *over there,* you need to use your imagination.

When you are feeling good and flowing your energy, you will know what action to take. You will be inspired from within.

Every subject has an emotional scale, which you can move up or down on.

You are playing all your "awake" subjects at once. This is the song you're sending out to the universe.

We want to move up the emotional scale in small steps so that it's comfortable and easy.

Remember the light bulb "glowing" over your head, with your energy flowing, and you feeling good.

11

The Choice Scale

Here we are at chapter eleven in a book about creating with the law of attraction, and we haven't yet asked a very basic question about all this. What do you want to create? What is the life of your dreams? If you're going to create this life, you have to decide what your dreams are. So, do you have dreams? Do you know what you want? If you do know what you want, that's great. You know what to do. Use your imagination, change your beliefs, and everything else we've been talking about so far. If you don't know what you want, that's okay; the world is set up in a way to help you choose and decide.

There are two ways for you to choose or decide what you want. The first way is simply for you to look around and pick what you like. This way works very well, especially when you understand how the law of attraction works and that you get what you focus on. You know that the universe is a universe of inclusion and that there is no such thing as no. You have your feelings to let you know when you're trying to say no to something. You remember that when you're trying to say no to something, you feel bad.

Our world is set up in an amazing way. Everything is set up so that you have a choice. The second way to chose involves, what

I call, the choice scale. The choice scale is as follows: choice / variety / difference /drama /turbulence. The choice scale has the parts of life that **cause** us to choose. For example, when something happens that we don't want, we learn from this more about what we do want. Let's say you're driving to work. You have an important meeting this morning, and you're ready and prepared. You left a little bit early, just in case. Then you get stuck in a major traffic jam. The longer you sit in traffic, the angrier and more frustrated you get. Do you remember what your feelings mean? The strength of your emotion equals the strength of your desire. So, while you are getting angry that you're stuck in traffic, you have a very strong desire for the traffic to be flowing so that you easily get to work. What did you learn from this? You learned that you don't want to get stuck in traffic. You know what you don't want. Now, let's focus on what you do want. *You want to be on time. You want traffic to flow so you can get to where you want to go. You want to be thought of as reliable and responsible. You want your clients to know you care about them.* Just from that one event, you've discovered four things that you want. If you really think about it, you could probably come up with a few more. I have a question: When you get stuck in traffic, do you sit there and get angry or do you imagine the traffic opening up and starting to flow again?

As I said, our world is set up to help us choose. That seems to make sense: If we're here to create, and we create by focusing the energy, then we need something to focus the energy towards. We have to decide what we want. The events and things that happen in our lives are there for us to choose and decide what we want. Are you starting to see how all this weaves together? I have said that in every moment and every situation you have a choice. Your choice is to be mindful in the now or not. You choose to create your life on purpose or to let it be created by default. You choose to focus on what you **do** want or to focus on what you **don't** want. Your feelings are with you every step of the way, always letting you know how you're doing.

I've also said that we are asking machines and that we are vibrating all the time. We are always playing a song inside of us, telling the universe what we want. We have always been telling the universe what we want when an event takes place in our lives. This is letting the events of our lives create our lives. This is also been referred to as living in reaction to what happens. We decide on a subconscious level what we want and send that information through our vibration to the universe. What you are learning here is how to move this to a conscious level so that you get to choose and decide, and you get to create what you want on purpose.

Everything is set up to give you a choice. Let's go back to the choice scale. The scale is: choice / variety / difference / drama / turbulence. Throughout this entire book, we've been talking about energy flow and being in tune with our desire. We've talked about creating friction in our vibration and how our beliefs filter our energy flow. The choice scale refers to how in or out of tune you are. In other words, the further up the choice scale you go, the more out of balance you are. When you're in choice, you are very much in balance and in tune with your energy flow and your desire, and you feel great. When you're in turbulence, it's like living in a small hurricane. You're way out of balance. You are not letting your energy flow, and you don't feel good. Let's visit the five stops on the choice scale so you get a better understanding about each stop.

Choice

The first stop is choice. Choice is the optimal state. You are in tune, your energy is flowing, and there's no friction in your vibration. You're paying attention to your feelings, and you are aware of how you feel. When you feel yourself getting out of tune, you easily bring yourself right back in tune. You very rarely live in reaction to the events of life. You realize that everything in life is a choice for you to choose what you like, and ignore what you don't like. You go around saying, "I like this and I like this and I also like this." If you begin to notice something you don't like, you simply change your focus. Your life is working. You're life is fun. You wouldn't change places with anybody, even if you could. When you're in choice, you could be feeling anywhere from contentment to joy to enthusiasm to excitement. That's a very large range, all on the positive side, so one specific example really isn't going to cover the range of choice. Let me give you a few examples that fall into this range. Do you remember earlier we talked about being in love? Not so much the light, floating feeling, but more of I'm in a good mood, and nothing is going to bother me. We also talked about, Leonardo DiCaprio in the movie *Titanic.* Feeling like the king of the world is certainly part of the choice range on the scale. You feel good. You feel happy. You feel confident. You feel like a kid again, alive, eager. When you feel like this, you are in the choice stop on the choice scale.

Variety

The second stop on our scale is variety. Variety is slightly different from choice because there's a little bit of friction in your vibration. On the emotional level, although the stop is still mostly positive, there's a little bit of a swing into the negative side. The ratio is probably something like 80% to 90% positive and 20% to 10% negative. You are usually in tune. Most of the time, your life is a joyous dance. You feel good, you're paying attention to your feelings, and your energy is flowing. Once in awhile, you let the events of your life create your life and live in reaction to them. Lots of things you want easily manifest in your life. You are in a good mood most of the time, and you are usually happy. An example of variety would be: You're driving along on the highway and traffic is easily flowing. You're easily getting to where you want to go. However, you are noticing a couple of negative things as you go, like another driver doing something that you believe is incorrect, like speeding, tailgating, weaving in and out of traffic, etc. Perhaps you notice some garbage on the side of the road. Maybe you see a lot of road kill as you're driving. When you're in choice, you tend to not notice any of the negatives and easily find things to appreciate, or you may notice something negative, but you easily ignore it and change the subject. When you're in variety, the difference is subtle. However, when you notice negative things, you're focusing on them a little bit.

Difference

The third stop on our scale is difference. You're having a pretty good time. However, you could easily go more negative or more positive. You're sort of on a tentative balance. Almost like walking a high wire. You're paying attention to what you're thinking and feeling about half the time. The other half of the time you forget to notice your feelings. The ratio for positive and negative is about 50%-50%. Half the time, you are living in reaction to the events of life. You are paying attention to how you're feeling more than you used to. However, if you still, occasionally, get ambushed by a complaining friend who saps your energy, and if you still, at times, get ambushed by the media by not paying attention to what you're watching on TV or by reading really gruesome things in the newspaper, then you are moving down the choice scale. However, you're also bouncing back up, so at times you feel like a ping-pong ball or like you are riding on a seesaw.

For example, you decide to go to the movies with a bunch of friends. The movie that you wanted to see is sold out. Most of your friends would like to see a horror movie instead. You don't like horror movies at all, and as soon as the thought of seeing one crosses your mind, you feel it in your gut. You feel scared and a little panicky. Your stomach gets a little nauseous. You feel cold and anxious, and the color drains from your face. But instead of paying attention to your navigation, your internal radar, you decide, with a little encouragement from your friends, not to be "a party pooper." You go and watch the film with them. The film is quite terrifying, and you feel terrible when you come out. Your friends appear a bit worse for the wear also. You do your best to enjoy the rest of the evening with your friends. However, you're still a little bit off. When the evening is over, and you're lying in bed trying to fall asleep, every time you close your eyes, you see the monster from the movie, and now you get mad at yourself. Why did I do this? Why did I go see that movie? I knew it would bother me. Why did I do that? Don't be too hard on yourself. You just created a much stronger desire within you, and next time, it will be much easier for you to decide not to go see the movie. This does take some practice. You didn't pick up all your beliefs at once, so you're not going to change them all overnight. As long as you're noticing how you're feeling and making adjustments accordingly, you are doing what you need to do.

Drama

The fourth stop on our scale is drama. Drama is mostly in the negative range. A ratio may be 75% negative to 25% positive. You tend to be negative more than positive. Your range, on an emotional level, may start at hope and go down to about anger, and sometimes dip even lower into hate. You only notice your feelings when they're really strong. Because of where you are on an emotional level, you usually have really strong negative feelings. A lot of your time is spent reacting to the things that happen in your life. You are running around putting out "fires" a lot. However, occasionally you remember to choose and create on purpose. We all know drama kings and queens. They are living their lives like they're caught in some kind of a soap opera. It's one thing after another, after another, and they say things like "I can't for the life of me figure out why my life is always such a mess." If your life is like this and you're reading this book, good for you, because if you follow what I'm telling you, your life as a drama king or queen will be over soon. If you know someone who is living like this, and they are your friends, and/or relatives, I suggest that you play in their dramas as little as possible, or not at all. If you're not paying attention to how you feel, then they can sap your energy and move you down with them. You do create your own reality. However, the people in our lives do have some influence on us. If you are happy going in to see them, when you leave, if you're lucky, you have only moved down one step. If you really buy into it and are supportive because you're "supposed to be", you may end up going way down into negative emotions. For example, you see someone who complains all the time, no matter how good the situation is, they always find something bad about it. Their life tends to be one problem after another. One day it's car trouble. Next they get stuck in traffic. They spill something on their brand-new shirt.

Their computer breaks down for no apparent reason. They can't find the remote for the cable TV. The longer you buy into their "stuff" the farther down on the scale emotional scale you go.

Turbulence

The fifth, and last, stop on our scale is turbulence. Turbulence is emotional high tide. You are way out of tune. You have some desires, maybe a lot of desires. But you also have lots of friction. Your beliefs are way out of line with what you want and are filtering out most of the energy. This imbalance of energy shows up in your physical body. You have headaches or indigestion, aches and pains and things like that. Things are way out of control. You are having a rough ride, to say the least. You definitely do not feel good. You are living your life entirely in reaction to the events that take place. Because your focus is negative, most of the events in your life are negative.

But now that you know what your feelings are for, you can start to bring yourself back in tune. The good thing about turbulence is that by having such a rough ride, you become much more focused about what you do want. Because when you're living something that you don't like, what you don't want becomes very clear to you. If you pay attention to this, you can figure out what you do want, like we did earlier in the story about getting stuck in traffic while going to work. You'll recall I said that we are always asking. When we are at emotional high tide, it's like we're screaming to the universe at the top of our lungs what we do want. Now, just because turbulence is a good thing in some ways, it doesn't mean that you want to keep living in it. Pay attention to how you're feeling and start making adjustments.

Review

Let's have a quick review: the choice scale represents how much of your energy you're allowing to flow. This is another way of saying how in tune or in balance you are with your desires and the energy you're directing through you towards them. When you believe you can have what you want, your belief is not filtering the energy at all. All of it is flowing through and you feel great. When you have a desire and you believe you can't have it but you want it anyway, your beliefs are filtering out most of the energy and this imbalance of energy feels bad to you. When this is happening, depending on how strong your desire is and how strong your negative beliefs are, you will move further up on the choice scale- maybe all the way to turbulence. As we change our beliefs and pay attention to how we feel about a subject, we move up the emotional scale to the better feeling emotions and that moves us down the choice scale towards choice. If we let our vibration, the song we are playing inside of us come from everything that we are observing in life, then our life tends to be inconsistent and bouncing up and down on both the emotional scale and the choice scale. When we start to control what we focus on and think about, which is creating on purpose, and pay attention to our feelings, then our life tends to settle down and flow much more smoothly. Keep in mind that we are never static on these scales, we are always moving up and down, sometimes a little bit, sometimes a lot. It took me awhile to learn that, because I tend to like things to go smoothly.

You're not being punished

I used to think the purpose of life was to make sure that everything went smoothly. Like living on a sheet of glass. No problems, no surprises, just everything flowing along smoothly and easily as planned. When it didn't, I thought I did something wrong and was being punished for it. I don't believe that any longer. Especially after I found myself off the road in the median in the bushes and trees after skidding off the road in a snowstorm. I'm fine. No one got hurt. The state police and the tow truck driver were very helpful. I greatly appreciate that. No other cars were involved. The only thing that really happened was that I was inconvenienced. I'm grateful because it could've been a lot worse. It was the day after Christmas. It was sleeting and snowing– not a nice day outside. I was angry because I had to open the store on a day I felt the store should have been closed. The bad weather also sneaked up on me. I didn't realize how bad it was outside when I left home. In that angry mood, I got in my car and started to drive to work.

I wasn't thinking or paying attention to how I was feeling. I had moved down on the emotional scale to anger and resentment. I had moved up on the choice scale to probably the lower end of drama. What happened was a match to my vibration, the song I was playing inside of me. I do now realize that a little rain falls in everybody's life once in awhile. The sun doesn't shine every day. Some days the sea is calm, and some days the sea is rough. That's okay, because from this experience, I much more strongly know what I don't want, and I much more strongly know what I do want. I really want to drive safely. I really want to pay attention to how I'm feeling.

The choice scale is another “scale” of life that we live in. As we find our gigantic orchestra inside of us, sometimes in tune and sometimes out of tune, we don't need to panic or freak out or wonder how or why we are getting this in our lives. We now know how to move back to choice. When we move away from choice, and "a little rain falls in our life," we know two things. First, the farther up we get towards turbulence, the stronger we are asking the universe for what we want. We more clearly know what we do want by living what we don't want. Second, we know we can easily bring ourselves back down to choice by paying attention to how we feel. With the exercises we've learned so far, and the rest of the exercises in chapter sixteen, this will be easy, but you have to do it.

Fingerprints

Do you know why we have fingerprints? No, not so the FBI can keep tabs on us. If our fingers were smooth, we wouldn't be able to pick anything up. Our fingerprints create a small amount of friction with the object we're trying to pick up. Without fingerprints, everything would just slide through our hands. The choice scale is the fingerprint of life. The choice scale guarantees that there will be motion forward. You remember in the beginning of the chapter I said our world is set up in a way that makes sure we are always asking. The choice scale is there so that we are always creating our life on a subconscious level to always make sure there's motion forward. This is Principle five: **You create your own reality, even if you don't know you're doing it**. That's how Principle five works.

Now that you know this, you have a choice to create your life on purpose or to let the events of life on the choice scale create your life for you. Either way is just fine. The choice is yours, there is no right or wrong in this. If you are living your life mostly in drama or turbulence you are not deliberately creating much at all. When you get yourself down the scale to variety and choice, then you are creating most of your life on purpose. You are consciously choosing and deciding, and what you want is easily flowing to you.

Are you beginning to see that you get to choose and decide everything? At every stop on the choice scale, you get to see what you're creating. If it's something you don't want, you are now much stronger. What does not kill us makes us stronger and more focused. From that, you also learn what you do want. The entire world is set up to give you a choice, and now you know how to choose on purpose. Most people let the events of their life create their life. Everything you've been learning in this book is to give you what you need to change your life. A life the way you want it to be, a life of your dreams. As we conclude this chapter, we've done some more fine-tuning. Having read this far in the book, you are realizing that you always have a choice. In the next chapter we are going to continue the choice theme. We are going to look at what is good and what is bad, and who gets to choose and decide. Knowing what's good or bad and who gets to choose would help you in your life, wouldn't it?

Summary:

You are here to create. What do you want?

The world is set up to give us a choice.

We are always choosing on a subconscious level and telling the universe what we want by our vibration.

We can live in reaction to the events of our lives, or we can consciously choose what we want.

The choice scale is so named to remind us **we always have a choice**.

The further up on the choice scale you are, the more contradictory beliefs you have, which is filtering out most of your energy flow. Hence, you feel bad.

When we live what we don't want, we more clearly know what we do want.

In everyone's life a little rain must fall. When it does, you now know to check your feelings and to reach to feel better. You always have a choice.

12

Good And Bad

What is good or bad, and who gets to determine that? You do. There is a line in *A Course in Miracles* that reads, "I have given everything I see all the meaning it has for me." You have a choice, in every instance, to decide for yourself whether something is good or bad, or to decide to take someone else's opinion of whether something is good or bad. We make judgments about everything all the time. The Bible tells us not to judge. However, we are taught to make judgments about everything. We've been taught to evaluate our lives and the lives of others so that we can be, do, and have what is right and what is good. We identify being right with happiness. We use our judgments as a way of trying to make us happy. Our judgments, hence a lot of our beliefs, are wrapped up in being right. This goes back to our early childhood where we were taught that being good is right and that being bad is wrong. Which in some cases was true and in other cases was simply someone trying to manipulate our behavior for their convenience or their own agenda.

Everything is neutral. We decide if it's good or bad, or we accept someone else's opinion. Now, this may come as a surprise to some of you. If you haven't come across this thought before, and you have never really looked at whether things are good or bad or neutral, you've probably just gone along with the prevailing wisdom of the times, never questioning the validity of good and bad. You recall from the last chapter that everything is set up to give you a choice–this includes what is "good" and what is "bad".

A lot of times we don't realize that we have a choice. I remember living on my own. I had moved out of my parent's house a couple of years earlier. I was talking with my friend Peter about going to work. He said to me, "Every day you have a choice of whether you go to work or not." I said to him, "No I don't." I was emphatic about it. My belief was that if you're not sick, you go to work. Period. There was no thought about it. There was no choice; you went to work. Then, finally, it dawned on me. He was right. Every morning I made a choice whether I chose to work or not. It was all in my control, and that totally blew my mind. I realized I had been indoctrinated into a belief that I had never even thought about, looked at, or questioned.

Positive and negative side

We can, if we want to, find the positive or the negative side of just about anything, and the prevailing wisdom will be evident no matter which side we choose. There is always plenty of evidence for either side. There are always two sides to every story. For example, "Don't talk to strangers," as opposed to "Always be polite. Say please and thank you."

Let's look at a few common expressions:

Time waits for no man as opposed to *stop and smell the roses.*

Don't sweat the small stuff as opposed to *mind your p's and q's.*

Clothes make the man as opposed to *you can't judge a book by its cover.*

An eye for an eye as opposed to *turn the other cheek.*

Early to bed and early to rise makes a man healthy wealthy and wise as opposed to *no rest for the weary.*

Here are a few good ones relative to work.

Having a job will give you experience, as opposed to *you can't get this job without experience.*

The early bird gets the worm, as opposed to *good things come to those who wait.*

Hard work builds character, as opposed to *why do it yourself, when you can have someone do it for you?*

Plan and prepare so you know what you are doing, as opposed to *just jump in with both feet.*

What about, *Nothing is free,* as opposed to *buy one get one free.*

Finally, *that's too good to be true,* as opposed to *I believe in miracles.*

From those examples, it's easy to see that cases can be made for either side of the good and bad coin.

Prevailing wisdom

People who make cases for one side or the other are known as spin-doctors. Their job is to put a positive spin on anything. However, they decide which side is positive and spin accordingly. They try to create prevailing wisdom. Prevailing wisdom is not always on the side of good. Prevailing wisdom tends to be either the loudest or the biggest group. Everybody else is saying it, so it must be right. This is the second of three chapters where the "subplot" or the "theme" is you always have a choice.

Here's an example: You're home sleeping, and at 1:30 a.m. your phone rings, and it's your teenage daughter calling you because she's been drinking. She feels that she's too impaired to drive the car home. She's calling you to come pick her up. This example perfectly illustrates that you evaluate every event, and then you have a choice. You decide what parts of it are good or bad, and if the whole event is good or bad. Ellen Langer says, "Events do not come with evaluations. We impose our evaluations on our experiences and, in so doing, create our experience of the event.[26]

Let's continue with our example. Is it good that your daughter decided not to drive? Is it good that your daughter was smart enough to call? Is it good that your daughter feels safe and trusts you enough to call you in a situation like this, rather than trying to drive? Are you happy about being woken up at 1:30 a.m.? Are you pleased that your daughter was out drinking? Before we can answer that, we have to ask, did you know your daughter was going to be drinking? Has anything like this ever happened before? On the whole, could this have turned out a lot worse? As you answer these questions, you are creating your experience of this event. From this illustration, you can also see that you always have a choice. Was this event good or bad? Only you can answer that, and you can only answer that for yourself.

Your own experience

Everything, and I do mean everything, is neutral, and we give it all the meaning that it has for us. We base our evaluations of an experience on our beliefs and our experiences. If we really look at this, we will see that it's our beliefs and what we've been taught that cause us to decide if something is good or bad. The event itself is simply the event. It's just something that happens. It's completely neutral. It's the way we look at the event that determines whether it's good or bad. Think about it right now. Can you think of any event that's not neutral? The answer is no. Everything is neutral, and something outside the event determines whether it's good or bad. Once again, you always have a choice, and you are always able to decide if something is good or bad. It's up to you.

Here's another example of this. Let's take a look at work. We all know people who love their jobs, and we all know people who hate

26 Langer, Ellen J., *On Becoming an Artist Reinventing Yourself through Mindful Creativity* Ballantine Books 2005

their jobs. Is it the jobs themselves or the people's beliefs about the jobs? Well, the person who's working at the job he hates is going to say it's the job. I know two teachers who both work at the same school with the same people, and even teach the same grade and subject. One of them absolutely loves her job. She is fantastic at it, has a great time, and the kids love her. The other teacher has been teaching for a long time. He's seen a lot of things change. He's had enough, and the only reason he's staying there is because he has tenure. He's not well-liked by the students. If you asked him, he would tell you he hates his job. So, which is it, if they both do the same job? It can't be the job, right? The job is neutral. It's their evaluation of the events that cause them to determine if they love their job or not. You also know by now two other very big players in this. One is the law of attraction, how each of them is vibrating, and what they are attracting into their lives. The other is where they are on the choice scale and how in or out of balance they are which also determines how they experience events. We determine for ourselves whether something is good or bad.

China

Here's another example of how our beliefs color our experiences. I had an opportunity to go to China a few years back. Marjorie went on a business trip, and I was able to go along with her. We saw some amazing things. We walked on the Great Wall. We saw the Forbidden City. We saw the Terra-cotta Warriors and many other things. One of the things that really struck me on this trip was when we went out into very small villages and got to see real China, not just tourist China. The people were living in what I perceived to be squalor, and we were staying in fancy, European-style hotels designed for foreign travelers. Our first reaction– this is terrible. Our second reaction– these people are happy. They had no idea what America is like or how Marjorie and I lived. Essentially, they were just living their lives. We both realized that we had put our standard of living (our beliefs) onto these people. They weren't having a bad experience. They were happy. Once we realized that and shifted our beliefs, we felt better too.

Judgments and reacting

Do you remember the first time you were in love? The joyful, sort of high-on-cloud nine feeling? You didn't care what happened or what events took place. You were in a great mood. You were on cloud nine, and nothing bothered you at all. What is the difference between then and everyday life? The answer is nothing. There is no difference. We can feel that way all the time if we believe we can.

We are taught to find fault. We are taught to judge, and we gauge those things we judge with our beliefs. Everything is neutral, and it's up to us to decide if it's good, bad, or neutral. When anyone but you decides what's good or bad for you, that's very disempowering; you don't have a say and that feels bad. Now that you know your emotions are the internal alarm system that tells you when something feels bad and to pay attention to that feeling, you will be aware of when this happens.

When we make judgments about things, we have to look into our beliefs and see whether it's the judgment or our beliefs that are causing us to be out of tune. You recall, back in the chapter on beliefs, I told you that a belief is nothing more than a habit of thought. We also have habits of reaction, knee-jerk responses that we automatically go into when our buttons are pushed. In reality, it's not the event at all. It's our reaction to the event. If it is something we care about, depending on how much we care, this will determine what kind of response and how much emotion will be involved in that response. Once you settle back down, you might want to take a good hard look at your beliefs and see if there's something there that needs to be shifted. In the future, if an event like that transpires again, you will not only know that it's completely neutral, you will have a choice of making it good or bad, right then and there. You will not be controlled by your conditioned responses. You will be able to choose how you will interpret the event. You'll live in the now instead of living in your reaction to the now.

Most people live their lives in reaction to what they see and to what's happening. It's the old, *tail wagging the dog.* Now that you know it's not the event, it is your reaction to the event, and your beliefs, you've taken a step into creating your own reality. With that, you'll start looking inside of yourself for the answers, rather than outside of you in the world. The heaven that you seek is within you. As we get to the closing chapters of this book, this is another main point for us to learn as we create with the law of attraction. Everything that we are looking for is inside of us. Our feelings are inside of us. Our imagination is inside of us. Our thoughts and beliefs are inside of us. Everything that we create starts inside of us before it manifests in the outside world. You do indeed give everything you see all the meaning it has for you.

As we wrap up this chapter, we are continuing with our fine-tuning. This chapter and the previous chapter were intended to build a strong foundation of choice. I hope that you're learning and understanding that you always have a choice. Because when it comes to the subject of the next chapter, most people don't realize they have a choice. In some cases, if they do realize they have a choice, it can still be hard to choose. The subject of the next chapter can reduce a lot of friction in your vibration. But you have to choose to do so. You understand that reducing friction in your vibration is a good thing, don't you?

Summary:

You are the one who decides what is good and bad.

We can find the "proof" of both the good side, or the bad side.

Everyone has his or her own experience of an event. The event itself is completely neutral.

We want to live in the now instead of our reaction to the now.

Everything we create starts inside of us from our thoughts, our beliefs, and our vibration.

13

Forgiveness

It's not a coincidence that this chapter on forgiveness follows the chapter on good and bad. As we just talked about, you give everything all the meaning it has for you. The same is true of forgiveness. You decide who and what bothers you and/or offends you. You decide what needs to be forgiven and what doesn't need to be forgiven. You also decide who to forgive and who not to forgive. This is the third chapter in a row in which I have been telling you that everything is set up for you to choose. You always have a choice. Even when it comes to forgiveness, it's you who decides to forgive somebody or to hold a grudge. A very important point to remember is that you're also deciding this about yourself. A lot of people have a hard time forgiving themselves. As we learned in the previous chapter, it is not the event. It's not what the other person did or did not do. It is our reaction to it and our beliefs about it.

I'm sure that you understand by now that our thoughts attract by the law of attraction, and that how we are flowing our energy determines whether or not the things we want are manifesting. Holding grudges or resentments stops energy from flowing. As we learned in previous chapters, when we allow friction in our frequency or vibration, we are slowing down or stopping the energy from flowing. This stops what we want from coming to us. Holding grudges and resentments always puts friction in our vibration and our song. Equally important, holding grudges and resentments always feels bad.

Holding a grudge

Let me get this straight. You're saying that if I'm mad at somebody, and I feel that they've wronged me in some way that I'm blocking my own energy from flowing? Remember, happiness is a feeling, and good feelings come when our energy is flowing. When we feel happy, our higher self is communicating to us that we are in harmony with ourselves, which means we are in tune with our higher self. We are in tune and in balance with our energy flow, which is flowing towards what we want.

By holding a grudge, you're playing two songs at the same time inside of you, and creating a whole lot of friction within you. *You're saying by not forgiving somebody that I am actually hurting myself?* Yes, that's exactly what I'm saying. An article from Newsweek, about the health of the body states, "Letting go of anger at those who wronged you is a smart route to good health."[27]

By deciding not to forgive someone or something, you are potentially choosing to damage the health of your body. Holding a grudge does not allow your energy to flow through you. The energy is life force. The sea of energy that we talked about earlier is the life force of everything– plants, animals, soil, air, water, and especially us. This is the energy that keeps us alive. Have you heard the expression "worried sick"? Well, you can also hold a grudge and make yourself sick. High blood pressure is an example of this. Your blood pressure gets elevated when you go into "fight or flight" syndrome. Fight or flight is a lot of chemical reactions taking place in your body when you perceive there is some kind of danger. Your blood pressure rises, your heart starts beating faster, and adrenaline is released into your system. High blood pressure

27 From Newsweek magazine, September 27, 2004. Article health for life. Forgive and let live. By Jordana Lewis and Jerry Adler.

can come from your body never fully releasing itself from fight or flight syndrome. Staying angry or mad and not forgiving can do the same. This is one way that holding a grudge or many grudges can affect the health of your body.

Remember we are talking about thought. A grudge or resentment is still a thought that you keep repeating over and over. You get what you think about. How you feel is your radar guiding you as to whether or not you're letting your energy flow. So, how does anger feel? How does resentment feel? How does being mad at somebody feel? How much energy do you want to waste by closing your heart? It's not natural. You have to work at it. Can you feel the effort it takes to stay angry? It's not natural for you to stay mad at your pet dog when he's done something wrong, if he comes up to you with those big sad eyes, and his head down. The same is true for everything else. It's not natural to hold a grudge and to stay angry. If it were natural, it wouldn't feel so bad. It wouldn't feel so empty.

Not letting my energy flow

Abraham-Hicks once asked me at a seminar, "How long are you going to be mad at this person and let him be the excuse for not letting your energy flow?" Then we all laughed as Abraham said, "Because right now it feels like you are going to be mad at him pretty much forever. You are going to use him as the excuse not to let your energy flow for the rest of your life, right?" From that I learned two things. First, that letting my energy flow was more important than holding a grudge. Second, which was even harder to swallow, was, even if I was right, letting my energy flow was more important. Did you get that? I was right! This person had clearly wronged me, I was right. But that didn't matter. By holding a grudge against him, I was not letting my energy flow. Let's review what that means. When you **are** letting your energy flow, **everything** you want is easily coming to you. What is everything? Everything is what you've told the sea of energy and the law of attraction that you want. What's **everything** to you? Health, well-being, focus, happiness, joy, love, fun, abundance, and we haven't even started on the material things yet. **Everything is every single thing that you want**, and by holding a grudge, you are not allowing it to flow to you. Are you getting that? Do you understand what Abraham- Hicks said to me? Do you understand what I just said to you? If you do, then you realize, **letting your energy flow is more important than any grudge could ever be**. You can easily see that letting your energy flow is also more important than being right. You've heard it enough times by now. Remember, do you want to be happy or do you want to be right? You know the answer.

Revenge

Forgiveness is almost a selfish act because forgiveness helps you. That's why we forgive. We always feel better when we forgive and let it go. Always. Confucius says, "If you devote your life to seeking revenge, first dig two graves."[28]

What do you think Confucius meant by this? To answer that let's start by getting a definition of revenge: Revenge: to inflict punishment in return for__________. Revenge, which we know is -8 on the emotional scale, means you are doing two things. First of all, you are holding a grudge. Second, you're not letting your energy flow. By not letting your energy flow, you are killing yourself, which is what Confucius meant when he said first dig two graves–because one of them is for you.

What do we do when we feel wronged? You remember what your emotions are, right? What does it mean when you feel bad? It means the thought that you are thinking, or what you are focusing on right now is blocking your energy from flowing. You know this because you feel bad, which is communication from your higher self. What do you do when you feel this way? You find a way to change the subject and focus on or think about something else. You learned earlier that this is a good way to change your vibration and the song you are playing inside. Then later, when you are feeling better and in tune, you can revisit the subject. You can decide what

28 From Newsweek magazine, September 27, 2004. Article health for life, forgive and let live. By Jordana Lewis and Jerry Adler.

to do and if it's worth stopping the life force flowing to you or not. I think you realize what we talked about earlier. The only option is to let it go, and I do mean actually letting it go, giving it up. Not holding it any longer, letting it completely go. Understand that I'm not saying you have to be friends with this person or socialize with them or anything else. The person I was speaking of earlier when I was talking to Abraham is not a friend of mine. If I never see him again, that will be just fine. However, if I do see him, it won't bother me at all because he is no longer my excuse for not letting my energy flow. I have completely forgiven him and let it go. Letting my energy flow is so much more important than being right.

Truth

Being right is also like trying to figure out what is true. There is a Zuni proverb that says, "There are no truths, there are only stories", which is an extension of the thought all things are neutral. If a lot of people agree about something, then we say it's true. But agreement doesn't make a truth. There are lots of different cultures around the world that do lots of different things. Some we agree with and some we don't. Is what we agree with true or truth? In some cultures, animals, that are considered pets in the United States, are considered food.

That brings us back to the conundrum. What is the truth? More importantly, who gets to decide? You get to decide, in every instance, for yourself, because all things are neutral. You decide if it's right or wrong, true or false, and if someone else has wronged you are not. If you don't decide this, there are plenty of people out there who will be more than happy to decide for you. You have been learning that everything you are looking for is inside of you. Your emotions are for you to navigate with. They are your internal radar. Your emotions are communications from your higher self to you, letting you know, in every instance, whether you're on track or not. This guidance from within is the only true guidance there is and the only real truth because truth is another thing that you get to choose. Nothing outside of you could possibly know what is best for you. Are you seeing that everything is set up to give you a choice? Are you also seeing that all of the answers are inside of you?

There's a quote from Eleanor Roosevelt, "No one can make you feel inferior without your consent." Well, I am going to change it just a little bit and say no one can wrong you, or "sin" against you without your consent. What do I mean by that? First, all things are neutral. "I give everything I see all the meaning it has for me."[29]

You recall that's our quote from the beginning of chapter twelve, *Good and Bad* in which we learned nothing is good or bad, it's up to us to decide. I think we have gone over this enough by now that you know it. And second, the key to all of this is that the law of attraction is taking care of everything. Nothing can assert itself into your life. You attract everything. If something occurs in your life, somehow, you are playing that song. You may not have known you were playing that song. You may have been playing that song by accident and not intending to, but if the event transpired in your life, somehow you attracted it. Now that you know that you are playing that song, you can change it to a different song.

Self forgiveness

As we conclude this chapter, I want to remind you that sometimes the hardest person to forgive is yourself. Because no matter how hard we try, we can't hide from ourselves. We can try to fool ourselves for a while. We can try to escape from ourselves through drugs and alcohol or other forms of addiction. However, in the long run, we really can't hide from ourselves. By not forgiving ourselves, we can become out of tune. In some cases, way out of tune. By our thoughts against ourselves, we don't allow our own energy to flow to us. This has a lot to do with our self-talk, which is what we say to ourselves inside our own heads. A lot of this self-talk comes from what we were told as children. Over the years, we repeated it to ourselves. Each time we did, the law of attraction got a hold of it made it a little bit bigger.

---

29 *A Course in Miracles* Foundation for Inner Peace. 1992

We have to find a way to forgive ourselves. We have to find a way to stop being so hard on ourselves. As some of these negative things keep coming up, we need to look at them and see if they are beliefs, and shift them. We need to look at our self-esteem and our self-worth and realize just how wonderful we really are. Right now, exactly as we are. The next chapter is called *Self-worth* and it's our final building block. It's the last note in our scale. With the previous building blocks that you have in place, you can do a very good job of creating your life the way you want. However, if you don't believe you are worthy, you will not allow yourself to have all that you've been creating. You do want to have what you been creating, don't you?

Summary:

You decide who and what should be forgiven and if you forgive them or not.

Holding grudges and resentments always puts friction in your frequency and puts you out of tune.

Holding grudges and resentments impedes your energy flow, which could harm the health of your body.

Do you want to be right, or do you want to be happy? Do you want to feel good and allow the things you want to manifest, or do you want to be right?

What is truth and true is subjective. You are the one who decides.

Our best guidance comes from within. That is what our feelings are and why we have them.

No one can "wrong you" without your consent. Everything is set up so that you have a choice in every situation. You always do have a choice.

14

Self-worth

Your self-esteem is based on your beliefs of how worthy you think you are. Everything in your life is affected by your self-esteem. Your job, how much money you have, and the lifestyle you maintain are all affected by self-esteem. The car you drive, who you date, where you live, the kind of house you live in. Your love life. The chances you will take, the things you will do in public. Public speaking, acting, singing, dancing, etc. What you will buy, how you will do in school, what kind of a career you will have, where you go on vacation. It has an effect on absolutely everything in your life. Most people today do not have a healthy image of themselves. If there's one thing that's greatly lacking in all people, it is self-esteem due to how we were brought up, society in general, the media, where we went to school, and what we were taught. Most of all our self-esteem is lacking because we have been taught to ignore our feelings and we have tried to guide ourselves from the outside rather than the inside.

I've spent a large part of my life trying to do something impossible. I've been trying to prove that I'm worthy. "If I do this then I will be worthy" was my motivation for a long time. The problem was that I was looking for an external measurement for an internal problem. Because when all is said and done, the only one who can decide whether or not I'm worthy is me. Nothing outside of me can fill a void that I feel within. The same is true for you. The only one who can decide whether or not you're worthy is you. It doesn't matter how you look, it doesn't matter what size you are, it doesn't matter how smart you are. None of that matters. As we've been talking about through this entire book, the only thing that matters is what you think. If you think you are worthy then you are. It's as simple as that. By now we realize it is important what we think, and we also realize it's important what we believe. What we have to do is change our beliefs about our worthiness. This is a crucial chapter because most people have low self-esteem and don't believe they're worthy. Hopefully, the information in this chapter will help to change your mind. Let's go back to the very beginning. We were on track when we were babies. We had great self-esteem. We had to learn the things that eroded self-esteem and got us off track.

Getting off track

How did all of us get off track? It all started when we were children. The negative conditioning began as soon as we were old enough to start moving around and getting our hands into things, and not just by the people who raised us but also by society in general. I have read that a child is told "no" approximately 60,000 times. Did you ever see a slightly older child with a younger sibling? The slightly older child tells the younger one "no" so easily. The conditioning doesn't take long. I understand there are safety issues here and that there are things around that are dangerous for babies. Maybe there's a better way than saying no to everything. Have you ever heard of the terrible twos? Where do you think they learned that? It's interesting, one of the first words a baby learns how to say is no. This is one of our first distortions because this is a universe of inclusion. There is no such thing as no. Everything is based on the law of attraction. So, instead of learning to shift our attention to something else, we are taught to try to say no to something. Innately, we know the truth. What do we do when the baby is reaching and grabbing for something that we don't want them to have? We show them something else. We wave a rattle or a teddy bear or something else in front of them trying to get their attention and trying to get them to focus on something else.

We are born completely whole, in tune with the universe, fully flowing our energy. We are totally empowered. Perfectly balanced between physical and nonphysical. We are wide open. We don't have any beliefs filtering our energy yet. We are in tune, which means in harmony with our higher selves and our energy flow. Picasso says, "Every child is an artist. The problem is how to remain an artist once he grows up." We are born perfect little beings. The problem is we are little, and we can't take care of ourselves. Soon enough, like everyone else, we get so distracted by what is here that we forget who we are. One of the purposes of this book is to help us remember who we are. In the book *Conversations With God*, God says, *"Yet, if you knew Who You Are-that you are the most magnificent, the most remarkable, the most splendid being God has ever created- you would never fear."*[30]

If you really want help with your self-esteem, write down that quote and remind yourself once a day. That's the way you were when you were born. You came into this life fully, completely, and totally worthy. Now all you have to do is remember that and believe it. I know this is easier said than done. But, right now, no matter where you are, or what you're doing, or what you look like, or what you've done, you are still completely worthy. Let's resume our trip from birth to adulthood and see how it affects our self-esteem.

Growing up

As we continue to grow as children, at some point, we begin to gain an understanding of ourselves. We also learn that if we think too highly of ourselves, and if we praise and compliment ourselves, we will be considered arrogant and egotistical. As we begin to get

---

30 Walsch, Neal Donald, *Conversations with God An Uncommon Dialogue*, Book 1 G.P. Putnam's Sons 1996

reprimanded by parents, teachers, and other children; instead of keeping a healthy self-esteem, most of us lower ourselves down to join the others. We begin to doubt our internal feeling radar and start looking outside of ourselves for guidance and approval. This is when we start to lose track of our navigation, which is guiding ourselves from within, with our feelings, hunches and inspirations. This doubt makes us vulnerable to the judgment of others, and then we start judging ourselves. This is when we begin to start feeling a void within us. Not understanding why we feel this way, we start looking outside of ourselves to try to fill the void. We also start questioning whether or not we can trust our feelings. This is also when our "self-talk" is starting to form. As I mentioned earlier, self-talk is what we say to ourselves. The most important thing I can say about self-talk is, **the only one who is listening is you, and you've been listening for your entire life**. Which brings me to the next point. What you say about and to your children becomes part of their self talk.

Not blaming

I've heard enough parents say things to me in front of the children and to children in front of me, that I guess they're not thinking about what they're saying. I also realize that these are probably things that were said to these people by their parents. I'm not talking about blaming anybody here. What I'm talking about is stopping and thinking. Is this really what I want to say to my child, knowing that a lot of what I say is going to become my child's self-talk? Which do you think is going to be better for your child's self-talk? When he's pouring a glass of milk, and he spills it, you say, "That's all right, just take your time. Next time I'm sure you will be able to pour it correctly." Or, "Why did you do that? You always spill the milk. Milk costs money. You're such a klutz." Equally important, what kind of relationship are you going to have with this child? When it's his turn, what is he going to say to his children?

Do you remember the first time your parent's words came out of your mouth? If you're like most people, it really freaked you out.

I remember one time I was baby-sitting for my younger brother. Although I don't remember the exact details, he wanted to do something. I said that he couldn't. At this point, he started to cry, and the next words that popped out of my mouth, shocked me as much as it shocked him. "If you wanna cry I'll give you something to cry about."

Speaking of what parents say, I was watching Oprah one afternoon. It was a special show with Oprah's producers talking about their favorite moments on the show. One young lady was talking about when Maria Shriver was on the show and how much it touched her. Maria said that every day she made sure to tell her children that she loved them and that they were terrific. She told them that they could be and do anything they wanted. What kind of a relationship do you think a parent will have with the child when the parent is encouraging the child and giving positive feedback? How do you think they're going to treat their children when they become parents?

What do you say to your children, besides, "no" 60,000 times? I'm guessing you probably want to balance that out somehow. Equally important, what do you say to yourself? We tend to be ruthless and overly critical of ourselves. If you want to improve your worth, what you say to yourself has to change. We talked about how to change beliefs and how to use your imagination. A little bit further along in this chapter we are going to be working on changing our self-talk. Let's resume our trip from birth to adulthood and see what happens when we get to school.

School

The next big surprise to our self-esteem is called school, where we find out that we are not considered amazing, wonderful, or individual beings. We are now going to be judged on our ability to conform to a standard created by a few. Now we find our worth being measured by tests and competition with others. Depending on how important the approval of others is to us, our desire for attention, and how willing we are to jump through their hoops, this can be a particularly difficult time in our lives. We learn hard lessons from looking outside of ourselves for guidance and approval. Competition is an interesting thing, because what it's supposed to do is prove one person is better than another. The entire premise is flawed. Because if you have to prove you're better by beating someone else at something, you're looking outside of yourself for approval, and you've lost touch with your navigation, your feeling radar. Another interesting thing about competition is it really has to do more with time, than anything else, because sooner or later everybody, no matter how skilled or not, can complete most tasks. However, it's usually the people who complete the task the quickest that are rewarded. I've heard football coaches say that the other team really didn't beat them, they simply ran out of time. Let's resume our trip and see what happens when we reach adulthood.

Looking outside

What are some of the things that can happen to us as adults if we continue to look outside of ourselves for guidance and approval? Well, we will search high and low, depending on how motivated we are, for that one thing that'll make everything all right: the perfect job, the perfect significant other, the perfect car, the perfect house, or the perfect shape and body size. Whatever it may be, the problem is, it's always the next thing. We never seem to find it. It's always just a little bit out of reach. Hopefully, at some point, we realize that there is no event that's going to come that will change our life so much that now we will feel good and be happy forever more. Happily ever after cannot be created by an outside event. There is no single event that is going to miraculously fix our life. Nothing outside of us can fill a void that we feel within. We have to choose to feel good and find a way to do that anyway.

What about the events of life? They are not going away. You're going to live on the choice scale, whether you like it or not. You can control where you are on that scale by how in or out of tune you are, but there will always be some form of choice, variety, difference, drama, or turbulence in your life. How much of it and how affected you are by it depends on what song you are playing inside of you, which is your vibration. You remember from chapter four that everything in the entire universe, including events, is a vibration.

Let's take a look at where most people are vibrating. Most people are well-meaning, but they are misguided because they are trying to guide themselves from the outside instead of from within. It's time for you to decide to guide yourself from within. We know what our feelings are and what they're for. The only way we are ever going to fill any void that we feel inside is from within. This can only be done by following the communication from our higher self, which comes to us in the form of our feelings. Nothing outside of us is ever going to fill what we feel inside. The emptiness that we feel, the void that I've been talking about, is our disconnection from our higher selves. Let's take it look at some subjects that we might feel a void about.

Outside control

Your body is something that you may feel empty about. Lots of people, especially women, are unhappy with the way they look. I have some great news for you right now. **You are not your body!** Remember back in chapter four, *Everything Is Vibration*? We are consciousness. We are energy but we are not our bodies. You and your body are connected, and you cannot be here without your body. Loving and caring about your body while you're in it is a good idea. You are inside your body, and you and your body are going to travel together through this life. But you are not your body. The media, to a large extent, has affected us about how we see our bodies, and about who and what is attractive and what is not. This is an example of guiding ourselves from outside instead of from within.

Let's take a look at this from a different perspective. Let's say you manufacture a product to sell to the public. You need a person or people to be seen wearing or representing your product. Who are you going to choose? There is lots and lots of money at stake here, so choose wisely. The answer should be obvious. You are going to find the most attractive people that you can. If you're selling clothing, you want to find people who look great in your clothes. If you're selling movies or TV shows, you're going to find the most attractive people you can find so you will appeal to the most people.

Suppose you're selling a product and doing just fine. Then someone tells you about this little trick. What is this little trick? Sex. Sex sells. Now you're going to find the best looking people you can find and have them wear as little as possible because your goal is to sell as much of your product as possible. Now there is actually nothing wrong with any of this. We know they do it. They do it because it works.

Where we run into trouble is when we compare ourselves to these "sexy" people. If only I looked like this, then I would feel good. If my body was like that then people would pay attention to me, and wouldn't that feel good. This is an example of choosing something outside of us, that we have no control over, to make us feel good. If you want to be in the spotlight, it has to shine from the inside of you out. We learned how to do this in chapter eight, *Imagination*. Instead of looking outside of ourselves for a way to feel good, we should look inside and feel good from our imagination and from our thoughts.

In school, we learned to compare ourselves to others, and to compete with everybody. This is where we ran into trouble. Because if we compared ourselves physically to someone else, and in our opinion, we didn't measure up, there's nothing we could do except for radical surgery. If our body structure or age or metabolism or height doesn't fit what the media's definition of attractive is, we are in trouble. We have disempowered ourselves by believing that something outside of our control determines whether we are worthy or not. Ask yourself, why am I comparing myself to others, and what am I trying to prove?

We were also taught to find our mistakes or flaws. We focused on these things and tried to fix them. This gave us a distorted view of things because we started to look for and focus on only what needed to be fixed or what was wrong. This began to set up a negative or fault-finding mindset. Which feels better to you? Feeling proud of the 75% you got right on your test or the 25% that you got wrong? A lot of people notice the parts of their body that they don't like. They start finding fault, looking for things that are bad, and pay more attention to that than the good parts. At this point, we all know about the law of attraction and what it does. You get more of what you think about. If you look in the mirror every day and say to yourself, "I am too much of this" or "not enough of that", you know by now, you get what you think. You also now know what your feelings mean. You know that when you're doing this, you don't feel good. I know this is easier said than done.

Start to change

Right now let's take a look at a couple of things that you can do to start changing this. The first thing to do is slow down the negative momentum. Every time you start thinking about your body, as soon as you notice, stop and change the subject completely. Say something like, "Just this one time I'm going to think about something else." Then change the subject. As you do this over the next few days, weeks, or months, you will stop thinking about your body, and you'll have stopped the negative momentum. Once you've gotten back to "neutral" and the negative momentum has cooled off, then you can start to change things a little bit at a time.

The next part is to find something to like about your body. There has to be something. Whether it's your hair or your eyes or your right arm. There has to be something. Your job is to find it and focus on it. Maybe it's your nose. Maybe it's your kneecap. Maybe you have nice toes. Maybe it's your teeth or your lips. Maybe it is that both legs reach the ground when you stand up. Whatever it is, find something, no matter how small it seems to be. This is only a starting point. The purpose of this is for you to start to appreciate your body, which will change the song inside of you that you're playing about your body. When you appreciate anything, you move up the emotional scale, and let more of your energy flow, which makes you feel better. As Lynne Twist wrote in her book, "What you appreciate, appreciates."[31]

31 Twist, Lynn, *Soul of Money Transforming Your Relationship with Money and Life* W.w.Norton & Co. Inc. 2003

I love that quote, and it's so true. It perfectly describes what the law of attraction does. When you think about your body, you are going to think about the things that you appreciate about your body, and those are the only things that you're going to focus on. It's just like we did when we created the affirmations. You only focus on the positive things about your body.

Your body is an amazing thing. You wouldn't be here if it weren't for your body because you cannot be here without your body. Isn't it amazing how you can eat food, and your body digests it, takes care of it, and knows what to do with it? Isn't your body amazing? It can breathe in air. It makes energy. How about your body's ability to see, hear, feel, and grow? Isn't that amazing? How about your body's ability to heal itself? Have you ever really thought about what an amazing, miraculous thing your body really is? You don't look like what's her name–so what? You're not the same size as so and so. Who cares? Did you read that quote from *Conversations With God?* **You are the most magnificent, the most remarkable, the most splendid being that God has ever created.**[32]

Do you get that? Do you understand what that says? You! Just as you are, right now, this very instant. You! The only difference between you and anybody else is the way you think and what you believe. It's time to change what you believe about your body and about yourself. Both you and your body are magnificent. Right now, exactly as you are.

You can see, by now, that comparing yourself to other people is very disempowering, which means, you have given your power away. All of your power is outside of you, and you are no longer in control. Now people can pull your strings, no matter which side of the comparison you end up on. It's also time for us to look at the evaluations of others and decide whether or not we are going to accept them because, once again, no matter which side of the evaluation you receive, it is still disempowering. What do I mean by that? As we take a look at this, we will see that the evaluation of others, whether positive or negative, is still outside of us and away from our own guidance.

---

32 Walsch, Neal Donald, *Conversations with God An Uncommon Dialogue*, Book 1 G.P. Putnam's Sons 1996

Evaluations

Our best guidance comes from within. However, we've been taught to accept the evaluations of others. We fall into this trap because of the way we were brought up. Through the school system we've become trained to accept the evaluation of others. The one thing that's not usually taken into consideration is the evaluator and what are his motives. Maybe he's having a bad day. Perhaps he doesn't feel well. Maybe he's under a lot of stress and pressure. Maybe he's prejudiced and doesn't like you for whatever reason. Maybe other things distracted him. Maybe he's completely misunderstood the point of your work and your praise or lack of it is based on this misunderstanding. Now, how valid is his evaluation? Maybe he's not willing to put himself aside and evaluate your work from an open objective place.

Imagine you are going into a college classroom for the first time. You're a student in your late teens. The teacher announces that he's a very difficult teacher. Because of the way he grades, 30% of the class will fail. Why does he do this? What is his motivation? Is he a bad teacher? Is he living off his past reputation? Does he believe he has a reputation to uphold? Has he ever worked in the real world? How does the college stand for that? You are paying this college a lot of money for an education. If this is the way things work, 30% of the time, they are not delivering what you are paying for. How many of you, as college students, would look at the teacher or evaluator and decide whether or not to accept this person's evaluation? How many of you would think about whether or not it's valid? The answer is, not many, because we're trained to accept other people's evaluations of us, especially in school.

Let's take a look at the positive side, which is an evaluator praising you. The same questions about the evaluator come up. Why is this evaluator praising you? Is it genuine, or do they have some sort of agenda? No, I'm not talking about being paranoid. My point is that if you rely on other people's evaluations or if you play the comparison game, your benchmark is always outside of you. Your benchmark is always out of your control. That is very disempowering. Enjoy the positive reinforcement that can come from evaluations and comparisons, if it's genuine. But if you rely on that for your self-worth, you're in trouble. Because no matter where you go or what you do, there is always somebody you perceive to be better. Approval is not something you can take with you. It can't be put it in the bank. You can't eat it. It's not a real thing. An artists who creates for his own sense of satisfaction, creates some of the best art; he is not concerned about the opinions of other people, positive or negative. He creates from his heart, and he creates what feels best for him and what he wants. I know plenty of artists and musicians who try to figure out what the next big thing is going to be. In other words, they try to create what they think the audience will like. Their efforts come up short. The work usually doesn't have the passion and emotion of work created by somebody who creates with their own sense of what feels and looks good. I know an artist who draws nudes very well. However, because of his upbringing, he rarely shows them to anybody because the appropriateness of this kind of work was questioned when he was younger. He is letting the evaluation of others keep his best work hidden from view.

Your approval and your encouragement should come from within you. That is the only way for you to be truly empowered. By empowered, I mean, your power is inside of you, and in your control. When you are totally empowered you are in tune, fully flowing your energy, fully connected to your higher self, feeling free and alive and vital. You are in the zone. When you are in this empowered state, the evaluation by others doesn't matter. It doesn't mean anything. You are as the universe created you, and you are the fullness of your being, like you were when you were born. I am not suggesting you reject genuine appreciation and praise. You should certainly enjoy it. Accept any positive feedback or encouragement. If it makes you feel good, it is good. Your feelings will never lie to you.

Self-talk

To get back to this empowered state, you need to change your self-talk, and you probably have to change some beliefs also. If your children or grandchildren are still small, what you say to them is the start of their self-talk, and you can have a big positive affect on them right now, if you choose to. As for yourself, you have to change your self-talk within you. Changing your self-talk is a good thing. It will not make you egotistical or arrogant. The first thing you want to do is to listen to some of the things you say to yourself, for a little while, maybe two weeks. Every day in the morning say, "I know what I say to myself is important. Today, as I go through my day, I'm going to really listen to what I say to myself and take note of it." The idea here is not to beat yourself up for what you're telling yourself. The purpose is to get an idea of what you are saying to yourself. A lot of people's running commentary is such a habit that they don't even notice it. In chapter sixteen, *Exercises,* we're going to learn how to meditate. Meditating is one of the best ways to stop the chatter in your mind.

After we have a pretty good idea what negative things we say to ourselves, the next step is to catch ourselves when we are doing it. No, not for the purpose of punishing ourselves. Each time we catch ourselves, we will smile or laugh because catching ourselves is a good thing, not a bad thing. We will say, "Just this time, I'm going to ignore that. Instead, I'm going to listen to 'I'm a good person'." After you've done this consistently, maybe a week or two, you are going to say, "I'm a good person, and I love me." Now I hear you all out there objecting. My question for you is if you don't love yourself, who will? After you've gotten good at doing that, you can begin to add your own positive statements to what you say to yourself. Remember back in chapter six, how we created our affirmations? You can start to use some of your affirmations here as a way of reprogramming yourself. Hold the image of a small child that you absolutely love and adore no matter what, coming home to you. You praise, approve, and love them, just because you do, not because of anything that they do, and/or achieve. You are this little child. If you can do this, you are well on your way to changing your self-talk, which will move you up the emotional scale. Equally important, you will feel better.

As I said earlier, self-worth is a very large subject that could easily be a book or two by itself. I hope this chapter has helped you and that you do the exercises included here. Your self-worth does affect every single aspect of your life. As you feel better about yourself and learn to love yourself, you will feel better. As you feel better, more of your energy will flow and as more of your energy flows, more of the things that you want will manifest in your life. When you know that you are worthy, you allow yourself to have, be, and do the things you want most from life. If you don't love yourself, who will? How can you really love anybody else, if you don't love yourself? I know how amazing you really are. The question is do you know how amazing you really are? It's not the conditions of things outside of us that control our lives. It's what we think.

As we wrap up this chapter, our final building block is in place, Principle nine: **You are worthy**. You now have all the notes that you need to change your life. As you improve your self-worth, and like yourself more, you will allow yourself to have more of the things you want. We are going to continue with our fine-tuning in the next chapter. Wouldn't it be nice if, somehow, you could control everything in your life so that everything would go the way you want it to? You wouldn't have to look within yourself to find joy and happiness because it would be all around you in your life. How do we control everything in our lives? The answer to that is the **title** and subject of our next chapter.

Summary:

Everything in your life is affected by your self-worth.

Only you can decide whether you are worthy or not.

We are all the most splendid beings God has ever created.

We are all born in perfect balance and are totally worthy.

The only one who is listening to your self-talk is you, and you have been listening your entire life.

The guidance and approval we are looking for is not outside of us.

We can change our beliefs and are self-worth anytime we want.

There is no event, or thing outside of us, that will "fix" everything so that we will all live happily ever after.

You are not your body! No one is!

Find things you like about your body and focus on them.

Living by comparison, or by the evaluation of others is disempowering to you.

Your approval and your encouragement should come from within. That is the only way you are truly empowered.

Everything you are looking for is inside of you. The heaven that you seek is within.

Changing your self-talk is good for you. It will not make you egotistical or arrogant.

Meditation is a great help in many ways. We will learn how to meditate in chapter sixteen, *Exercises.*

Do the exercises to change your self-talk, which will change your self-worth, and you will feel better.

15

You can't control the world.

Are you a control freak? Or, just a bit of a controller? Do you like things to go your way? Do you want to be right more than you want to be happy? Do you feel better when everything is "under control"? Do you feel all right when things are going the way you want and feel bad when they don't? Do you worry or panic when things don't go your way? The belief behind this is if you could control everything, you would feel better. You're right. You probably would feel better. Deep inside you know that feeling good is the key. Now that you have read this book, it is not deep inside anymore. It's right out in front in your consciousness. The only problem with this plan is that you can't control the world.

As I was saying at the conclusion of the last chapter, if we can get everything in our lives under our control, then we wouldn't need to look within or pay attention to our feelings. There would be no motion forward, and we would all be bored to death. I've said that everything is set up so that you have a choice. To have a choice, there has to be things that you want and things that you don't want. You'll notice I didn't say things that you say "yes" to, and things that you say "no" to because we know there's no such thing as no. The only way to say no to something is to not pay attention to it–to change your focus to something else. You remember all of that, right? Without lots of choices and variety for you to choose from, you wouldn't be able to create all that much. For example, let's say you are a master artist, and you are ready to paint, but you only have three colors. Not the three primary colors either. Yes, you are a master artist, and with those three colors you can probably create some amazing things. But imagine what you could create with endless color choices. If we could control everything in our lives, we would only choose the things that we like that feel good and eventually end up with very limited choices. The universe is not set up this way. The universe is based on abundance. That's why we have everything we need inside of us.

Being guided by fear

When you don't know why you are getting what you're getting because you don't know about the law of attraction and the way the universe is set up, you can end up being guided by fear. What does that mean? If a lot of things are happening in your life that you don't want and you think are bad, you become fearful of the world. You try really hard to say no to the things that you don't want but that doesn't seem to work either. All of you, by now, know why. The only logical thing that you can think of is, somehow, I must control the world, so that these bad and fearful things don't come to me.

If you don't know that everything you need is inside of you, then the only logical conclusion is to try to control what's outside of you. It makes sense to try to control the world or at least your little corner of it. Because if you don't know that your thoughts create and you don't know what your feelings are for, the outside world appears to control you and you're always living in reaction to what's happening. You cannot control the world. No matter how hard you try or how big and strong you get, you just can't do it. People have been trying to control the world since the beginning of time. No one has succeeded.

Let's take a look at some of the things we do to try to control the world. Look at laws. There are lots of laws in this country, and they're making new ones all the time. Are laws successful controlling people? The answer to that is obviously no, because if that were the case, there would be no crime, and we know crime is still happening. Some of our laws come with very strong and severe punishment. In some cases, even death. That still doesn't stop people from breaking the law. The law does not control them. I realize this may appear to be a little bit black-and-white here. But I am not talking about people, I'm specifically talking about the laws. Laws were created to try to control people and the world. Do the laws control everybody? The answer is no.

Influence

Is there anything out there that successfully controls everything? The answer to that is no. There are people and organizations that have very strong influence, but they can't control everything. There are people out there who are trying to control their world by influencing and controlling you. Some of them made influencing you an art form. They use very powerful persuasion and influence techniques on you in attempts to get you to do things, like buy their products, and get you to give them your money. They are trying to control their world by controlling you. In some cases, they are using the law of attraction. They may not realize what's behind it that makes it work. But you and I know it's the law of attraction.

You remember how the law of attraction works. Whatever you give your attention to gets bigger. Whatever you give your attention to, you attract more of. There are a lot of people out there who want your attention. Do you watch television? The people who are creating advertising, television shows, and commercials are powerful influencers. They are using the law of attraction, but they're probably not aware of that. The commercials are designed to get your attention, and then they show them to you again and again and again and again. You know whatever you give your attention to, you get more of. That's the whole premise behind advertising.

Television advertising or commercials are great example of this. Did you notice that television commercials give you a problem first and then miraculously fix it? Let's take a look at an example. The commercial starts off by telling you it's a certain illness season again. Insert whatever illness you want. Then they go into a very strong description of how bad it feels. We all know how important feelings are. Then they tell you that you don't want to have to deal with it again. It was really bad. Unfortunately, you have no choice. It's that illness season again. They don't know that nothing can assert itself into your life. Then just by chance, they have this amazing product that will fix you up in a jiffy. You'll be just fine. The question here is does the commercial make you sick? The answer is *if you focus on it enough, it might.* You know what the law of attraction is and how it works. You also know that you can't say no to something you don't want. The only thing you can do is focus on something else. You see how they are using the law of attraction. They get your attention and get you to focus on a commercial for more than 17 seconds and then they repeat the process by showing the commercial again and again and again. If you watch television, remember that you have a choice to mute the commercials.

Other forms of media also try to get your attention and influence you. Do you watch the news? Do you read the newspapers? The media uses sensationalism and slants the stories to fit a certain point of view. They use the excuse of "you need to know what's going on", and most people mindlessly follow. Let's take a look at their business, and don't kid yourself, it is a business.

The news business

Here we are in the news business. We have a product to sell, whether it's our newscast, newspapers, show, or other form of media. It is still a product. There are lots of things out there in the world that are trying to get your attention. There is lots of competition for your attention because step one in influencing you is getting your attention. There are hundreds of channels on television now. There are countless numbers of publications and newspapers. What do we do to sell our product to you? First, we find the best looking, most articulate people that we can put on the screen in front of you. Then we have to come up with some really juicy stories that get your attention, hold your interest. For some reason, I don't know if it's force of habit or just human nature, but negativity sells. If we can find a negative story and make it sensational, so it gets and holds your attention, now we are influencing you. If you keep watching our newscast or show, you're buying our product. If you keep reading our newspaper, magazine article, etc, you are buying our product. This makes our sponsors and us happy. We have successfully influenced you.

Let's take a look at an example to illustrate this point. This is a story that was reported by the media. It is negative and was sensationalized to get and hold your attention. Since the turn of the new millennium, there has been an "outbreak" of a new deadly disease that is going to go quickly around the world and cause an epidemic. I don't want to give this any extra energy, so I'm not going to name the disease. If you really want to know, it won't be that hard for you to figure it out. The world population as of September in 2005 was 6,466,258,575.[33]

That's almost 6.5 billion people. The population of the United States is 297,152,953. That's almost 300 million. In 2003, this dreaded disease had 8098 reported cases, mostly from Asia. If you try to make a graph showing the population of the world versus the number of people who got this disease, the amount is so infinitesimal that you cannot even put it on a graph. If you used only the population of the United States, it's still not going to graph. Why do we need to know about this? We don't. It's about holding your attention.

The population of the five largest cities in the United States is: New York, 8,104,079; Los Angeles, 3,845,541; Chicago, 2,862,244; Houston, 2,012,626; and Philadelphia, 1,470,151. I'm going to include Boston because I live near Boston, which is ranked 24th in population with 569,165 people.[34]

If something happens to 10 or 20 people in any of these cities, compared to the number of people who live there, why do we need to know about it? If you look at what they report compared to the

33 US Census Bureau 2005

34 US Census Bureau 2005

number of people who live there, there's really no comparison. What I want to do is make you aware that these things have some measure of influence upon you, depending on how much you pay attention to them, which gets the law of attraction involved.

Feeling vulnerable and frightened

Is this what you want to give your attention to? Do you want to be influenced by the news and the media? Does this mean that I don't care about my fellow man and that I have no compassion for the things that happen to other people? Of course not. Everybody is living somewhere on the choice scale and that's how they are creating their reality. My question is how does watching the news **make you feel**? Do you feel safe and secure? How does learning about all these bad things happening to other people affect you? All this does is make you feel vulnerable and frightened. Watching the video of a disaster, over and over, is that going to help somehow? If you don't feel like a victim, keep watching, you will soon enough. We have two things to think about here. First, how does it make you feel? Second, what are you giving your attention to? You know by now, what the law of attraction does and what your feelings mean. Do you still think watching the news and reading newspapers is a good idea? I don't. I haven't for over 20 years. Fortunately or unfortunately, if something bad enough happens, I hear about it without the aid of a newscast or newspaper.

Paying attention to the news and the media can cause you to develop a negative mindset. Earlier in the last chapter, *Self-worth,* I talked about how we start to develop a negative mindset. We focus on what's wrong or what needs to be fixed. I used the example of a test score where you got 75% right and then you focus on the 25% that you got wrong. This is part of the reason why so many of us become faultfinders. We think that there are many things in this world that need to be fixed, removed, or changed. In every case of the above examples, we are focusing on the problem. "One cannot solve a problem with the same kind of thinking that gave rise to that problem." Albert Einstein. In truth, nothing really needs fixing. This is a hard thing for us to learn. The best way to fix something is to stop paying attention to it. This is why there is no such thing as negative publicity anymore. You've all seen the stories. Something negative happens to someone who's a celebrity, and instead of hurting their career, it only makes them bigger. We know what the law of attraction does. By focusing on the problem, we are making the problem bigger. We should imagine a solution, instead of focusing on the negative, the problems. If you can't think of what the solution might be, then turn it over to the universe and asked the universe for help or to take care of it. Some people call that prayer. The most important part in all of this is to stop focusing on the problem. It's hard at first, but it gets easier and easier with the help of the law of attraction.

What can I control?

Even with the law of attraction we can't control everything in the world. We have some influence upon it, but we can't control it. Others really can't control us either, as long as we're focused on what we give our attention to. What exactly can I control? The only thing you can control is you. That's the only thing you need to control. No one can create your reality except you. Only you create your life and your world. You do it by what you think and what you pay attention to. You know how you're doing by how it feels. What you want to control is not the event, it's your reaction to the event. You choose what you think about and focus on. When something doesn't feel good, you now know to think about something else to change the subject to focus elsewhere. In any given moment, there are a myriad of things that you can focus on, whether they are right around you or in your imagination. You control your focus, and you control what you pay attention to, which controls how and what influences you and what you influence.

As we conclude this chapter, we have done some more fine-tuning. We have learned about our influence and the influence of other people. We've also learned that we are the only ones who can create our reality, our world. You have all your building blocks in place. You know all the notes to the scale, and now you can create whatever music of your life you want. In the next chapter, you will learn some more exercises that will sharpen your focus, show you the law of attraction at work, and give you the practical things that you can do to change your life. Some exercises to do this would be helpful, wouldn't they?

Summary:

You cannot control the world. Guide yourself from within, instead of being guided by the things you fear, which is outside of you.

Be aware that others are trying to influence you and decide what you give your attention to.

Pay attention to how you feel when you watch the news or read the newspaper?

Notice what gets your attention.

Remember, everything is set up for you to choose. You always have a choice about what you give your attention to.

Even with the law of attraction, we can't control the world and other people.

16

Exercises

Let's start this chapter with an overview of the exercises. The exercises will help sharpen your focus, show you the law of attraction at work, and give you some practical things that you can do to create the life of your dreams. There are nine exercises. Do the law of attraction exercise first. After that, you can do the rest of them in any order that you like. You can start with the ones that interest you the most, and then move on to the rest. Exercise nine, **The Energy Scale**, is a very powerful and important exercise. You use this exercise to shift your beliefs and help move you up on the emotional scale. This exercise can create some big changes in your life. Remember to refer back to this or any exercise when a situation arises and you want to deliberately focus or shift your energy. I still do some of these exercises every day. These exercises will help you whenever you need them. The key to this is *doing* them. They can't help you if you don't do them. The exercises are as follows:

1. **The law of attraction exercise.** This exercise will show you that the law of attraction works and that you are using it every day, all the time.

2. **The count your blessings exercise.** This exercise will help you appreciate people, things, and moments in your life. When you are vibrating or playing the song of appreciation, you are the closest you can be to your higher self. You are in tune.
3. **Meditation.** Meditation is a great way to stop mental chatter and quiet your mind. Meditation also raises your vibration.
4. **Breathing exercise.** The breathing exercise will help you feel better in your body and help your energy flow freely.
5. **Make your own music mix.** Music helps to make you feel good and lift your spirits.
6. **I appreciate**. This exercise also helps your appreciation. When you are vibrating or playing the song of appreciation, you are the closest you can be to your higher self. You are in tune.
7. **Ben Franklin revisited.** This exercise teaches you how to look at only the positive side of things and helps you develop a positive mindset.
8. **Hey, I thought that.** This is another law of attraction exercise that shows you how your thoughts are energy and how similar thoughts attract each other.
9. **The Energy Scale.** This exercise helps you move up the emotional scale and helps you shift beliefs. This is a very important and powerful exercise.

A lot of these exercises are designed to create your future. I want to remind you to remember your "now". If you live too much in the future, you lose your now, and you don't necessarily get the future either. All your power is now. Some focus on the future is good but stay in balance. Stay in tune. Here's an affirmation: *I am happy with my now and eager about what's coming.* When you are doing these exercises, you may bring up old beliefs. Sometimes bringing old beliefs forward and shifting them can move us up on the choice scale a bit further out of tune. This is not a problem for two reasons. First, the further up on the choice scale we go, the louder we are telling the universe what we want. Second, we know how to move ourselves back into balance. Exercise nine, **The**

Energy Scale, is a great exercise for helping you get back in tune and in balance. We are going to move forward as our life changes and old beliefs fall away, which will raise our vibration and help us create what we want. Have fun and enjoy these exercises.

1. The law of attraction exercise.

The first exercise I want to talk about is for the law of attraction. It's easy and will show you that you do create your own reality. Here's how it works: I want you to think about a song you haven't heard in awhile. Preferably a song you like. Think about why you like it. Do you like the words? Do you like the rhythm? Do you like the way it feels? What is it about the song that you really like? Can you remember the last time you heard it? Do you know all the words? Do you like to sing along with it? Got it in your mind? Can you hear it? Good. Now I want you to say out loud, "I want to hear this song. Bring this song to me". Yes, you are asking the universe to bring this song to you. Did you say those two things out loud like I asked you to do? When you think about something, you are giving your attention to it, and you are focusing the energy. You are asking the universe for it. When you ask out loud, your asking is more focused. When you write it down, your asking is the most focused. That's why I will have you write things down in some of the exercises coming up.

The first time I did this exercise I wanted to hear *Round and Round* by Ratt. I like that song because I think it has the best dual guitar solo I've heard. I think the harmonies are terrific on the solo. Being a guitar player– that's probably why I like it. I did the exercise in the morning, and later that day, I was in a store and I heard *Round and Round*. Within a couple of hours I heard the song I wanted to hear. I knew I was creating my own reality.

If you honestly did what I asked you to do in the first paragraph and answered those questions in your mind, and actually listened to the song in your head, and thought about it for at least 17 seconds, then before long, when you turn on the radio, the stereo, or the TV, you will hear your song. The *Round and Round* story is from the first time I did this exercise, which was quite a number of years back, when I first learned about the law of attraction and how it works. The story about Anna Nalick's song in chapter three happened within the last year while I was writing this book. Years later, asking the universe to play a song for me, as you can tell by the Anna Nalick story, worked very well.

Okay, let's try something else. We also talked about cars in chapter three, *Law Of Attraction.* When you buy a new car, all of a sudden, you seem to see that car all over the place. If you haven't bought a new car recently, pick a model and a color of a car that you would like to see and think about it. Is it a sports car? Is it an SUV? Is it a sedan? What color is it? Think about these things. Decide what car you want to see, and then say, "I want to see this car. Show me this car".

We can have a little more fun with cars. My birthday is June 18th. I decided I would like to see my birth date on car license plates. I thought about it a little bit, which started the energy flowing. Now everywhere I go, no matter what part of the country I'm in, I see my birth date on license plates. I also see my initials (EJL), or I see my name, Ed. You can do the same thing. It's relatively easy, as I've explained. Just thinking about it– which is asking- starts the energy flowing. "I want to see my initials on license plates. Universe, show me license plates with my initials on them". Before too long, you will see them.

Here are a couple of other things you can try. What's your favorite color? Say, "I'd like to see the color red. Universe, show me red". Think about your favorite color, which starts the energy flowing. Before long, you will be seeing your favorite color all over the place. Is there a bird or animal you would like to see? Just think about what it is and put some energy into it and keep your eyes open. You'll see it. You can do this with just about anything. That's a good start to show you that the law of attraction works and that you are indeed creating your own reality.

Just a reminder, your thoughts have to be clear thoughts. You remember clear thoughts from chapter five. Your thought has to be a single vibration. If your thought is two vibrations, then the thought is not clear, and the two vibrations cancel each other out, so nothing seems to happen. A clear thought is the thought that has only one vibration and is focused for 17 seconds, with strong desire, and feels good. You remember this from chapter five, right?

2. The count your blessings exercise.

The next exercise is called count your blessings. It's been around for a long time. I'm sure most of you know it. The question is have you ever tried it? This is how it works. Get a notebook or a journal, and write down your blessings. For example:

I am blessed because__________.

I am grateful for____________.

I love to____________,

Or, what felt good today? Then list the things from today that felt good.

The good things about______________ are_____________.

I feel good when I______________.

Choose one of these as your subject and start writing. You can do this a few different ways. You can write five things a day at the end of the day before you go to sleep. For example, just before you go to bed at night, you would write, "I am blessed because" and then list five reasons why you are blessed. You can do it first thing in the morning to start your day off right. You can just write them when you feel you need a pickup, a boost of energy. It doesn't have to be great, big events. Just look for some things that feel good. By focusing on things that feel good, you will feel better also. You can do all six from the list above everyday or just one. You are more focused when you write things down. However, if you don't have access to paper and pencil, you can do this in your head. If you want to do it while you are waiting in line or have a few spare minutes, that's a good idea. The purpose of this is to help you feel better. We all know by now what our feelings are and why we want to feel better. These are basically some ideas to get you rolling.

3. Meditation.

Meditation is a process of deep relaxation and gently quieting the mind. As we talked about in the earlier chapters, this is a great way to quiet the chatter in your mind. It does take some practice and does not happen overnight. If you work at it consistently, then you'll find that it helps you in many aspects of your life. I've been doing meditation for well over 20 years. At this point, I can't imagine living my life without meditating. I started meditating for spiritual reasons and then quickly found out that meditation also has many health benefits. For example, "Brain Check" an article in *Newsweek* from September 27, 2004, says, "Research at Harvard suggests that the relaxation response, the deep sense of calm we can achieve through yoga prayer or simple breathing exercises, can help counter the effects of chronic stress."[35]

Meditation is a combination of all those. You'll feel a deep sense of calm and relaxation, and you will control your breathing. All of which will have a positive effect on your body and your mind. Read through the directions first and then try meditating. You can try it right now. Any time that you want to meditate is just fine (except while driving).

When you meditate you want to be consistent. If you decide to meditate in the morning, try to do it at the same time every morning. The time of day doesn't make a difference. It's the doing of it that makes a difference. There are many different ways to meditate, and they're all slight variations on the same theme. Here's the basic way to do this:

Find a quiet place where you won't be disturbed for about 10 to 20 minutes. I recommend that you sit. Eventually, you will be able to meditate lying down. In the beginning, when you're just learning, if you are lying down, you are probably going to fall asleep.

You also want to wear comfortable, loose fitting clothes, so that you do not feel them and are not constricted by them around your body as you meditate. Place both of your feet on the floor, and place your hands gently in your lap. If your arms or legs are crossed, uncross them.

Close your eyes, take a deep breath in through your nose, and slowly exhale through your mouth. Repeat this three times. Take another deep breath, and as you are breathing out mentally repeat to yourself the number 3, three times. Take another deep breath, and as you exhale, mentally repeat to yourself the number 2, three times. Take another deep breath, and as you exhale in through

35 Benson, Herbert, M.D., Julie Corliss and Geoffrey Cowley,, *Brain Check* Newsweek article, September 27, 2004

your nose out through your mouth, mentally repeat to yourself the number 1, three times.

Now, we are going to relax and go a little bit deeper. We are going to count from 10 down to 1. We are going to say to ourselves we want to go as deep as we possibly can but stay awake. As we count from 10 down to 1, with each count, we are going to say to ourselves "relax and go deeper".

At this point, we're going to let our breathing return to normal, which will be gentle and relaxed, in and out through the nose. When we get down to 1, you should be in "a meditative state." Your brain will be in one of the four following rhythms, depending on how deep you actually got: alpha, beta, theta, or delta. As you practice this over time, you will be able to get all the way in to delta just about every time.

Now that you are in the meditative state, you have a couple of choices. First, you can gently concentrate on your breathing, slowly in and slowly out, not too deep and not forced. Just gently notice how you are breathing and try to hold your attention there.

What's going to happen, especially if you're just beginning, is your mind is going to wander. You are going to start thinking all kinds of thoughts because it's finally quiet, and all that stuff inside your head wants to be heard. That's just fine. Whatever thoughts come, just relax, meditation is to get you away from stress, not to cause it. The answer is to always just relax. It's just fine. When you realize you've drifted, gently bring yourself back to noticing your breathing.

The more you practice meditation, the easier it will become. Your mind will get quiet, and all the chatter will eventually just go away.

Now, I said you had some choices. You don't have to focus on your breathing. If you prefer, imagine something and hold it in their mind. If you are going to do this, it has to be something simple. The whole point of this is to stop thinking. Choose something like an apple or an orange or a tree or a flower. Something simple that doesn't take a lot of concentration.

Another choice you have is you can focus on a single tone, like a musical note, hum to yourself and say the word "om" or "ah". Another way you can meditate is gently repeating a word to yourself. Try: love, peace, joy, happiness– anything along those lines. I know this sounds a little bit complicated, but if you read it through a couple times before you do it, you will easily understand the process.

When you decide you are ready to come out of your meditative state, count to three, and say the following to yourself: "At the count of three, I'm going to open my eyes, be fully awake, and feel great. One, at the count of three, I'm going to open my eyes, be fully awake, and feel great. Two, at the count of three, I'm going to open my eyes, be fully awake, and feel great. Three, eyes open. I'm fully awake and feeling great."

It wasn't hard to do, right? You can stay in your meditative state for anywhere from five to 15 minutes, depending on your schedule.

A few additional thoughts while you're meditating. If you get itchy, go ahead and scratch because you'll get more distracted trying to ignore the itch than if you just went ahead and scratched, so scratch. If you have to check to see what time it is, then only open one eye. If you get completely interrupted, then you should count your way back in and re-relax yourself. Also, tell yourself that sounds and noise only help you relax and go deeper.

A few other thoughts about meditation: Remember earlier I said I would tell you about an exercise to help you fall asleep? The exercise is to count your way into the meditation as we just went over. However, you tell yourself that this time, you are going to go all the way into sleep. You have a couple of options. You can count down from 25 to 1, or you can count from 10 down to 1. When you are finished counting, if you are still not asleep, gently say and repeat to yourself "relax and go deeper". Then pause, breathe gently, and repeat to yourself "relax and go deeper". Keep doing this til you fall asleep. It sounds more complicated than it is. It works. However, if you're new to meditating, it may take a little more focus and some practice. Once you've become used to meditating, this will be very easy for you.

4. Breathing exercise.

How many of you pay attention to how you are breathing during the day? If you paid attention to your breathing, you would notice that your breathing changes depending on your level of stress during the day, how you feel, and how well you can stay in balance. If you get scared or frightened, you tend to hold your breath. If you could see what you were doing, you would notice, as soon as you found relief, that you would start breathing deeply again. When you are nervous or worried or anxious you breathe shallow and quickly. That's better than holding your breath but still not great.

Former concert guitarist and teacher, who heals people with the powers of breath, Andy Caponigro says, "Breathing blocks are the resistance we create against our own feelings. These attempts to block unwanted feelings by interfering with the movements of our breath are the source of every bit of self-conflict and doubt we experience in life."[36]

We all know how important our feelings are from chapter two, *Emotions.* By not knowing what our feelings are and what they're trying to tell us, we can use them to interfere with our breathing as Andy just said. This only makes us feel worse.

Breathing freely and normally will make us feel better. Here's another exercise that deals directly with breathing. You can do this once or twice a day or when you notice your breathing is out of its natural rhythm.

It's very simple: Sit like you're going to meditate (same position of hands and feet), and breathe in slowly and deeply through your nose, and slowly exhale through your mouth.

As you slowly exhale, breathe out as much of the air as you can, try to empty your lungs. Do not bend over or squeeze your rib cage or anything like that. Just naturally exhale as much as you can, and then inhale as deeply as you can, through your nose.

Do this three to five times, and then just let your breath return to its natural rhythm. If you've been stressed, nervous or anxious, this will make you feel better.

---

36 Caponigro, Andy, *The Miracle of Breath, Mastering Fear, Healing Illness, And Experiencing the Divine* New World Library 2005

If you want to learn some more breathing exercises, the information about Andy's book is listed in the bibliography.

5. Make your own music mix.

I believe everybody has his or her own favorite music and favorite songs. These days it's easy for people to make a music mix. They take all their favorite songs and burn them onto a CD or put them onto an MP3 player. I want you to do the same thing. I want you to pick your absolute favorite songs– the ones that make you feel really good when you listen to them. Whatever kind of music that makes you feel good: Country, Rock, Blues, Jazz, Gospel, Soul, Rap, Hip-Hop, Broadway show tunes, Classical music, Opera, New Age, whatever it is. Feel free to arrange the music anyway you want; this is going to be your mix. This is for you only, and it doesn't matter if anybody else likes the music or not. You want the music that whenever you hear it, you feel better. Then I want you to make your own mix onto whatever you have, CD, cassette tape, whatever. Whenever you're feeling a little blue, I want you to listen to your mix. On your way to work in the morning on your way home at night. When you go to see the dentist, whatever it might be. Whenever you're feeling down, play your mix. If singing along with it makes you feel better, then sing along with it. Keep listening to it until you feel better. If you have enough music that you love to make more than one mix, go right ahead. The purpose of this exercise is to use music to deliberately raise your frequency and make you feel better.

6. I appreciate.

This exercise is similar to the count your blessings exercise. Pick a subject and write down everything that you can think of that you appreciate about the subject. The subject can be anything. It can be a person. It can be something that you like to do. It can be a pet. It can be a plant or a flower. It can, literally, be anything. Let's look at a couple of examples:

I appreciate this beautiful morning. I appreciate the golden sunlight shining through on me this morning. I appreciate the gentle breeze. I appreciate hearing the birds sing. I appreciate seeing all the beautiful plants around me. I appreciate seeing the beautiful blue sky. I appreciate seeing those white puffy clouds.

Let's try another. I appreciate my wife and the things she does to make my life easier. I appreciate the way she does her half of the chores. I appreciate it when she makes dinner for me. I appreciate the way she makes sure I present my best self to the world, not going out with two different color socks on. I appreciate that she calls me to see how I'm doing. I appreciate when she surprises me with unexpected things.

I appreciate everybody who helped me with my book. I appreciate my editors. I appreciate my publisher. I appreciate my wife who helped me create my book. I appreciate everyone who reads my book. I appreciate everyone who does the exercises in my book. I appreciate everyone who buys my book. That's you! Thank you! I really do appreciate it.

When you are appreciating, you are letting your energy flow fully, and you are in the moment. If you're really feeling it, it's a perfect blend between your self and your higher self. You are, in that moment, who you really are.

A variation on this exercise would be to do it inside your head. That way you can do it anytime you want, no matter where you are. Whenever you see something that you appreciate make note if it. If you're standing in line, look around for, remember, or imagine things that you appreciate.

7. Ben Franklin revisited.

You remember the Ben Franklin exercises from chapter six, *Beliefs*. This is a good exercise to help you change your vibration about someone you're not getting along with. Whether they are giving you a hard time, are hard to live, or work with, you can change the song inside of you that you are playing about them. This will change your vibration, so that the next time you interact with them, things will go much better.

To do this exercise, get out your sheet of paper, write the (+) plus sign on top of it and write the person's name next to it and then list as many positives as you can think of about them. The more the better. Try to fill the page. It can be anything as long as it's positive. For example:

He always dresses well.
He likes to cook.
He does try to do the best that he can.
He can be very helpful when he wants to.
He has a very nice speaking voice on the phone.
I appreciate the fact he usually leaves me alone.
I can see that he usually means well.
He is usually very punctual and doesn't keep me waiting.
He really does love his children.

I think you're getting the general idea. Fill the page. If you do this, the next time you interact with this person, it will go much better. You can do this with anybody. It doesn't have to be somebody you are having difficulty with. This will raise your frequency about anyone.

8. Hey, I thought that.

This exercise, based on the law of attraction, shows you how your thoughts attract. To do this exercise you need a small notebook, and you need to keep it with you. Throughout the course of the day, every time something that you have been thinking about comes up in your world, write it down. For example, you're thinking about somebody and they call you on the telephone. Another example of this would be when you are talking to somebody and you both say the same thing at the same time. You can use the things you thought about from the law of attraction exercise- license plates, songs, cars, etc. Once you start writing these things down, you are going to be amazed at how often the things that you're thinking are coming up, all around you. I think on my best day I had 25 to 32 things that I was thinking come up in my day. Most days, it was somewhere around 15 things that came up.

9. The Energy Scale.

The Energy Scale is an exercise that helps you move up the emotional scale. You can use it to help you feel better. You can use it to shift your beliefs. If you find you have a belief that keeps coming up, this is probably the best exercise to shift the belief and to move yourself up the emotional scale about that particular subject. Depending on how strong your belief is will determine how many times you have to do this exercise. If it's not that strong a belief, once or twice may be enough to completely shift it. If it is a strong belief that you've had for a long time, you may have to do this exercise quite a few times. Each time you do it, it'll raise you up the emotional scale, and eventually you will have shifted the belief completely. As we do this exercise, we want to pay attention to how we feel. We are looking for thoughts that feel good.

To do this exercise, you need a blank piece of paper. At the top of the paper, you are going to write what it is you want to shift. For example, I want to reach to feel good more. Another one would be, I want to know that I am worthy. Start writing a thought that you believe about this subject that feels good to you. If you come up with a thought that you don't believe or doesn't feel good, don't write it down and try again. As you start this exercise, you may go through a few thoughts before you find one that feels good and gets you started. That's perfectly fine. Just keep looking for a thought that feels good. As the energy starts to build, it gets easier and easier. Just like in the affirmation exercises, the energy will probably be subtle in the beginning. So you have to pay attention to how you feel. As you start moving up the scale, you will feel the momentum building, and it will be easier to tell if a thought feels good or not. Let's look at a couple of real-life examples that I actually did to help me feel better and shift some of my beliefs.

At the top of the page, I wrote: "I want to reach to feel good more."

I am understanding that feeling good has benefits.

I can see that feeling good can help me.

I like when I feel good.

I can see that things go better when I feel good.

I am starting to understand that when I feel good my energy is flowing.

I'm starting to understand that how I feel is important.

I am starting to understand that how I feel is my radar.

I do see that things go better when I'm in a good mood.

I know that my feelings have meaning.
I understand that reaching to feel good will help me.
I know that it's up to me.
I know that I can choose my own song.
I know that I can choose what I focus on.
I know good things happen when I feel good.
I have seen what feeling good does.
I am finding it easier to find thoughts that feel good.
I do want to feel good.
I love to feel good.
I believe I can do this.
I know with parctice I can do this.
I know I can remember to reach to feel good.
Why not feel good!
I feel better already.
I've decided to reach to feel good.
I've decided to choose more often what I focus on.
I've decided that I can do this.

As you read this, you should feel a subtle (or not-so-subtle, depending on your frequency) shift in your energy. I still do every time I read it. If you get to the bottom of the page and still have more ideas flowing, simply turn the paper over. If you have really got it flowing, and you really feel good, use as many sheets of paper as you want. The purpose is to raise your frequency on the emotional scale. If you're feeling it, keep doing it.

Let's do one more.

At the top of the page, I wrote: "I want to know that I am worthy."

I can see the beauty the universe has created.
I can see that I am part of what the universe has created.
I can see the good in all that the universe has made.
I am starting to understand that all of us are part of this good.
I am starting to understand that I am also part of this good.
I am starting to understand that I am worthy.

I am starting to understand that I do not have to prove anything to anyone.

I am understanding that the universe see me as worthy.

I understand that we all make mistakes and that's how we learn.

I understand that man measures by what we do not who we are inside.

I feel that I can see myself as worthy.

I am starting to feel better about this.

I can see that because I am, I am worthy.

I feel better about me.

I know that success does not guarantee feeling good.

I know that measuring success is about ego not worthiness.

I know the universe sees me as being worthy.

I can feel that worthiness comes from within me.

I am starting to see myself as worthy.

I am starting to believe that it's about what I think about me.

I am starting to believe that I choose whether I am worthy or not.

I am starting to believe that this is inside of me, and not up to the world to choose.

I believe that I can choose worthiness for myself.

I believe that this is an internal choice.

I've decided to think of myself as being worthy.

I've decided that it is up to me whether I am worthy or not.

I've decided that I am worthy.

I've decide that I am going to be kinder and more loving to myself.

I've decided that I am going to take better care of myself.

I have decided that I am worhty.

I hope you can feel your energy shift from that one. Worthiness is really important to everyone. I hope you do these exercises and enjoy them. They will work if you do them. If you want to feel better, do the exercises. If you're interested in more energy exercises, I highly recommend the book *Ask and it is Given* by Esther and Jerry Hicks. This book has 22 exercises that will move you up the emotional scale and raise your vibration or frequency. Information is listed in the bibliography.

As we conclude this chapter on exercises, I want to remind you about the exercises that we learned in the previous chapters. In chapter five, *Thoughts,* we learned what a clear thought is and how to create one. A clear thought is a thought that has only one vibration and is focused for 17 seconds, with strong desire, and feels good. In chapter 6, *Beliefs,* we learned how to create a new belief in 30 days. We learned the "Ben Franklin close", and how to create affirmations with it. In chapter eight, *Imagination,* we reactivated our imagination and learned how to visualize. Remember to start by asking questions. In chapter fourteen, *Self-Worth,* we learned about our self-talk, and what we say to ourselves is important. We did an exercise about the body and learned how to change our self-talk.

I have put together all the knowledge in this book to help you change your life. These exercises will have a definite impact on your life and your reality. It would be interesting to see how this works in reality wouldn't it? That's what we are going to talk about in the next chapter. These events are from my life, and you'll be able to see how this works.

17

Does This Really Work?

At the end of March 2005, on a Wednesday morning, I drove to work. I worked at a rug store, which meant working every weekend. Mondays and Tuesdays were my days off. I live south of Boston and drove on three highways, 495, 95 and 128 to get to the store. My morning commute, depending on traffic, could take anywhere from 55 minutes to an hour and a half. As my co-workers and I drove in, we called each other on our cell phones to let each other know how heavy the traffic was and when we thought we would get to the store. Joe, who lives north of Boston, called me as I was driving in to let me know that the traffic was heavy north of the city. He doubted he would be in by nine o'clock. He also wanted to let me know that two people were laid off the night before, and that the overall mood of the company was somewhat tense.

Traffic wasn't that bad for me that morning, and I made good time getting to work. I was early enough that I was able to go pick up Zeke, a co-worker at the train, which I did when I was early or when it was raining. As we drove to the store, he also told me that two people were laid off last night. I jokingly said to him, "I wonder if they will lay me off too?" We both had a good laugh about that and talked sports until it was time to go into the store.

When we get into the store, I put my stuff down. The boss said he wanted to talk to me. I said sure and followed him back to his desk, thinking that he was going to tell me about what had transpired the night before and that morale was kind of low. Perhaps he would talk about what we were going to do about it. As we sat down, I noticed he was very nervous. He said to me, "We are letting you go." I was quite surprised, and I think I said something like, "Huh?" To which he gave another short explanation and asked me if I wanted to clean out my desk now or come back some other time. Sitting there in complete shock, I was able to say that I would clean out my desk now, not wanting to have to drive back there ever again. Everybody I worked with was just as surprised as I was. Quite a few people thought I was kidding, until they looked at my eyes and saw the hurt. Here I am, right in the middle of writing this book, suddenly, without a job in a questionable economy. This is a disaster.

Or is it?

Our story actually starts quite a few months earlier. My wife, Marjorie, came to me and said, "I want us to have a day off together." I said, "Okay, that is fine. Pick the day that you want to have off together, and we will make plans to do what you want to do." She said, "No, that's not what I mean. I want us to have a day off together every week." "That's impossible," I said to her. "With the work that we both do, unless one of us changes our job that's just not going to happen." Marjorie is an Oriental rug buyer for a retail chain and works six days a week. Monday through Saturday. I'm working at the rug store, and I work five days a week. Wednesday through Sunday. So we haven't had the same day off together in over six years.

I asked her what she wanted to on this day off together? "Go to art galleries and look at paintings," she replied. "I also want to go to the art museums that we haven't been to in a while. Visit some of the local art areas that we haven't visited on Cape Cod. I also want to go back to Newburyport and to Rockport and places like that." "That's fine," I said. "Sounds like a lot of fun, but to do that, one of us is going have to get a new job." To which she replied, "I knew you were going to say that, and you are right, one of us needs to get a new job."

New job

Can you guess which one of us got to look for a new job? If you guessed me, you would be right. For lots of reasons, and without focusing on the negatives of that job and you know why not to do that, I started looking for new job. We decided that I would wait til the spring to find one. I got laid off at the end of March. Does that sound like the spring to you? Next, I started writing in my day timer, universe, please bring me a new job. I told my parents I was looking for new job. I made a list of the nine things that I wanted in a new job. I got an index card, and I wrote across the top of it; what do I want from a new job?

1. To be appreciated and respected
2. To earn more money (I did write a specific amount).
3. An easier commute.
4. An eight-hour workday.
5. To be able to get the days off that I want.
6. To be off some or all weekends.
7. To work with good positive healthy people.
8. Something fun and interesting that I enjoy.
9. Minimal lifting, if any at all.

I put that card in my pocket. I would try to read it once a day.

Most of those are self-explanatory. Everybody wants to work somewhere where they are appreciated and respected. All I am going to say about that is, it is not a coincidence that it's number one on my list. Earn more money, that one is obvious. Easier commute, I live approximately 40 minutes away from the store. However, during rush hour, that can be anywhere from an hour to an hour and a half as long as there's no Patriots game or a concert at the Tweeter Center on my way home. On Wednesdays, the store was open from 9 a.m. till 9 p.m. Add on the two-and-a-half hours of commuting, and let's just say, as far as I was concerned Wednesdays didn't exist, especially in the winter. I left in the dark and came home in the dark. When you work in retail, the busiest days of the week are generally Saturday and Sunday. Those are the days when you are going to make most of your money. You want to be there on the weekend. This can be a problem when you need a weekend off or when you want to get certain days off. Number seven is not a knock on the people who work there. Some of my friends are still there. If you are going to work someplace, you want the frequency or song to be positive and healthy. You want that to be the song of where you are working. Number eight is also self-explanatory. The average 9 x 12 handmade rug weighs between 50 and 100 pounds–that relates to number nine. The larger rugs weigh even more. So not only was I working at a rug store, I was also lifting weights.

Basically, the song that I was playing about working in the rug store was: I've had enough of this, and I'm ready to go. Maybe I had stayed longer than I should have, or more likely the universe had everything perfectly under control, as far as timing, matching my song, Marjorie's song, and when it was time to leave. One of the other things that I had not mentioned is that we also needed to have some work done around the house. We were doing a small kitchen renovation. We had redecorated the dining room already. Now, we were going to do the upstairs bedrooms, making them into offices and more usable space for Marjorie and me. As it turned out, I was able to do most of the work myself because, suddenly, I had the time to do it. You know from what we learned about the law of attraction that there is no such thing as a coincidence. Had I left the rug store after finding a new job, I wouldn't have given myself any time to do any of the work around the house. I would have just gone straight to the new job.

After two weeks of painting, I got back to writing this book. The painting proved to be very therapeutic. I felt really good, and I was in the zone and enjoyed writing. After about another week or so, we were both concerned about our finances, and at that point, I told Marjorie I would have a new job within two weeks.

The following Sunday, I get the newspaper. Before I had a chance to go through it, Marjorie went and circled about a dozen ads for me. The first ad was about selling advertising for an art publication. I wasn't exactly sure what that was. A number of years ago, I had answered an ad where they wanted me to sell, let's say, cheap and tacky paintings out of the trunk of my car. I couldn't tell much from the ad itself and figured it must be something like that. Marjorie convinced me to fax my résumé to them anyway. I could always say no. I also contacted the other 11 ads from the paper. Can you guess what happened? You're right. I was hired by the art publication.

The job consists of going to art galleries, museums and art associations, telling them about our publication, and making it available to them to advertise in. My territory is eastern Massachusetts, Maine, Vermont, and New Hampshire. I get to schedule my own time. I can travel when I want, (not during rush hour.). Basically, I get to spend my days talking to people and looking at great art.

Marjorie's song

Let's go back and look at my intentions for a new job, and Marjorie's intentions for the two of us together. First, let's look at Marjorie's. She wanted us to have a day off together so that we get to do things that we enjoy. Being able to schedule my own time, I was able to choose to work or not on Sundays. Finally, after almost 7 years, we had a day off together. Another thing that we were able to do is see galleries and art museums. We would go together. Although technically I was still working, we got to spend a day together, looking at art, seeing some of the places that we love to go to, and enjoying a nice lunch or dinner together. The universe delivered us an exact match to the song Marjorie was playing.

My song

How did I do on my intentions? Let's go back to my index card that I kept in my pocket. Number one: I wanted to be appreciated, and respected. The folks at the art publication have appreciated my efforts and shown me respect at every turn, which I really appreciate. Remember the exercises from chapter sixteen, **I appreciate**. You recall that's a very important exercise. An appreciation always connects you to your higher self. Number two: was about how much money I wanted to make. We will see how this pans out as time goes on. Number three: an easy commute. Although, at times, I drive much further than to the rug store, I also have control over what time I drive. I don't get stuck in rush-hour traffic. Number four: eight-hour days. With this job I can schedule my own time. If I want to work later, I can. My schedule is entirely up to me. Number five and six: we were able to get the time off to go to Texas for my niece's graduation from high school. Working retail, getting to family functions had always been difficult, especially the ones more than halfway across the country. We were able to go to Texas, and we had a blast. Number seven: I wanted to work with positive, healthy people. I pretty much answered that in number one. These folks are great to work for. Number eight: being an artist (a painter) and a photographer, going to galleries and museums is a perfect match for the song that I'm playing. Lastly, number nine: although I do carry some paperwork and copies of the publication with me, it's nowhere near lifting a 100 pound 9 x 12 rug. The universe matched everything on my list. The universe heard the song that I was playing and played along.

Playing our song

As you can see, getting laid off was actually a good thing. It was the universe joining together in the songs that Marjorie and I played. The universe played along with us perfectly. In other words, the universe matched our frequencies perfectly. In chapter twelve, *Good and Bad*, we talked about the fact that we give every event all the meaning that it has for us. If I had decided that getting laid off was a bad thing and let the song that I was playing be negative, none of this would have worked out the way it did.

As for right now, working for the art publication will keep my interest. However, life is a journey, and with every new situation that comes along, we adjust the song inside of us that we are playing. In other words, we change our frequencies. Life is a journey and an adventure. What I really want to do is teach the information in this book and write more books. Not to mention create and play music, draw, paint, and take lots of photographs. I will be at the art publication for a while, but it is just a step on my way to what I want to do. Just another step on the journey and adventure that is my life.

Don't Miss the Point

If you are expecting a story about a "giant step" then you missed the point. It's not that giant steps can't or don't happen or that giant steps have not happened for me because they have. You'll recall from chapter ten, *Giant Steps,* that giant steps can be uncomfortable and disconcerting. But more important than that, if I had told you a story about how my life was utterly transformed by this amazing giant step, you would think something like, "Well that's great for you, but I can't do that." If you don't believe that you can do this and that it will work for you, you're right: you can't and it won't.

You have to believe that you can do it or it will not work for you. The story I just told is about small easy steps. If we look at the story and see how everything worked out, even the things that appeared to be bad, you will realize how amazing this is. It's not about creating some big giant step every once in a while. It's about creating your life every day and manifesting the everyday stuff. And yes in time you will be able to manifest "big things", however they will just be the next step and not a giant step.

As you begin to work on this by doing the exercises, paying attention to what you're thinking and feeling (the song that you're playing to the universe), and changing your beliefs when necessary; you will see your thoughts manifesting in your life. You will make the connection between your thoughts and your emotions. You will watch your everyday life unfold. You will know that you are doing this. You will become more confident, and believe and know that it works. That's when you will truly become the creator of your life and that's the point that I don't want you to miss. It is the small easy steps. Pay attention to the song that you're playing to the universe. Watch it manifest. Make the connection that it does work. You can do it. And you are doing it.

18

Coda

"Man's mind once stretched by a new idea never regains its original dimensions." -Oliver Wendell Holmes.

Four Reasons

The title of this book is *Creating With the Law of Attraction: 10 Principles That Will Change Your Life.* To create something you need to want to create it. To change your life you need to want to change it. In chapter eleven, *The Choice scale,* I asked you what you wanted to create. What do you want? In this the final chapter, I'm asking you to again think about what you want, as we look at four reasons that prevent people from creating, changing, and getting what they want.

What prevents people from creating what they want? Having read this book, you know the answer. The only thing that can keep you from your dreams is you. There are four reasons, and, hopefully, this book has helped you with three of them. One of them is entirely up to you. The four reasons are as follows:

People don't think they're allowed to choose what they want.

People don't know what they want.

You focus on too much of what is getting your attention and not enough on imagining what you want.

You give up too soon.

The first reason people don't think they're allowed to choose what they want is because they have low self-worth or self-esteem, as we talked about in chapter fourteen, *Self-Worth*. They have negative beliefs about themselves. They don't think they're good enough or have the talent. We know that desire is much more important than talent, so if you have strong desire, you're asking the universe for what you want. Also, they are afraid to make a mistake. They are afraid in general. They don't think that they are worthy. They're concerned about what others think.

These are all simply negative beliefs, and they all can be changed. There are three exercises that are specifically designed to help you with this: A new belief in 30 days from chapter six, *Beliefs*; improving your self-talk from chapter fourteen, *Self-Worth*; and exercise nine, The Energy Scale from chapter sixteen, *Exercises*. I hope that you did and/are doing the exercises so that if you have any of those beliefs listed above, you are in the process of changing them.

The second reason is people don't know what they want. This is the one that's entirely up to you. This book will help you with the other three reasons, but I can't choose and decide for you what you want. The only way for you to get what you want is for you to decide what it is you want. Just know this, you are only limited by your imagination. You can have anything you can imagine. You are worthy of anything you want, and if you don't believe that, work on the three exercises listed in the previous paragraph.

The third reason, and this is where a lot of us fall down, is that you focus on too much of what is getting your attention and not enough on imagining what you want. Nothing seems to change. Your vibration is too much about everything that's going on around you. Hence, you're not sending the signal of what you want enough. You don't have to spend hours and hours imagining. Just a little bit of imagining, 30 seconds here and there will help. Ten minutes a day will have an affect on your life. I've talked about the fact that each of us is playing a song inside of ourselves. The universe hears the song, joins in, and plays along with you. The universe does not know if the song is about right now that you are living or something that you are imagining. Start playing the song of what you are imagining, and play it because it's fun and because you enjoy it. Remember feeling good is the key. When you were a kid and you were daydreaming, you were daydreaming for the fun of the daydream, not to try to make something happen.

The fourth and final reason people don't get what they want is that they give up too soon. We've all heard stories about musicians who went to every single record label twice before they got a deal. Can you imagine how strong the desire is to get a record deal after being told no so many times? Why did they finally get a record deal? Two reasons, first they finally got their vibration or frequency clear enough to get what they wanted. They stopped playing two different songs inside of them at the same time. For example, we really want to get a record deal, but we're not sure we are good enough. You can see that there are two different songs or vibrations going on at once there. We talked about clear thoughts in chapter five and in the last chapter. A clear thought is a thought that has only one vibration, is focused with strong desire, and feels good. The universe could finally, clearly hear their song and join in and play along with them. Second, their desire was strong enough. They were focused enough that they did not give up. Don't give up too soon. What we've talked about in this book does work, and it will work for you if you believe it, so believe it and keep going. If you keep going, sooner or later you will believe it, and the universe will get you what you want

The universe is taking care of everything and the timing of things, matching all the songs you are playing inside of you. Matching how to give you what you want. As you just read in chapter seventeen, *Does This Really Work*? I could not have possibly figured out the details of leaving one job, painting the house, spending time with Marjorie, getting a new job, etc. by myself. Yet, it easily flowed together when I was open and allowed the universe to take care of it.

It's written in The Bible that faith the size of a mustard seed can move mountains. A mustard seed is really small. Creating what you want, and using the principles in this book does take some faith to trust that the universe has everything under control and always has your best intentions in mind. I can only speak from my experience and say, as far as I'm concerned, the universe always does. Faith is a personal thing. I recommend that if you need to, you work on yours. Don't give up, keep imagining for fun, and enjoy the vision of your goals. Sooner or later, it will manifest.

A final thought

Am I using the law of attraction? Am I changing my life? Am I creating what I want? The short answer is yes. The long answer is also yes. Every day I'm living some of my dreams. Just about every day I have new ones. Some are manifesting now, some will manifest tomorrow and the next day. Some not for many years yet. I am still getting into them, tuning and adjusting the song that I'm playing, there is no ending to any of this. Every time the universe matches our vibration or frequency, and something manifests, we start composing a new song. Life is a journey. There is no "done". "Done" is a concept that we learned from school and from how we were brought up. Is your homework done? Are you done with this? Have you finished what you are working on? You never finish the requirements to complete your life because there are no requirements for you to complete. Your life is not something that you can get done. If you have been waiting to get it done first, it's time to stop waiting and start living. Doesn't eagerness and excitement about the future, knowing there is more fun to come feel better than waiting? We all know how important feeling good is.

How many people do you know who are living the life they want? The answer to that is obviously not so many. To which I say, try the principles and exercises outlined in this book. You have nothing to lose and everything to gain. What's the worst that can happen? You feel a little better. You enjoy life a little bit more. You can continue to live an unsatisfying life, or you can become really good at this and create the life of your dreams.

The only true measure of success in life is joy. How much joy are you living? How good do you feel? No matter how happy you are, you can always be happier. The emotional scale has no top to it. There is no limit to how much joy you can live.

I am wishing you all the monetary and material abundance that you could possibly want. But more than all that, and more than anything else, I wish you all the joy you can handle and then some.The law of attraction has put this book in your hands, and I appreciate your reading it. I know how powerful this material is. I know this works. Now it's up to you.

Bibliography

A Course in Miracles, Foundation for Inner Peace,1992 ISBN 0-9606388-8-1

Arntz, William Chasse, Betsy Hoffman, Matthew *What the Bleep Do We Know?* Movie DVD 2004 Captured Light, and Lord of the Wind Films LLC.

Bass, Ronald *What Dreams May Come* Movie DVD 1998 MCA Home Video Based on Novel By Richard Matheson

Caponigro, Andy-*The Miracle of Breath* Mastering Fear, Healing Illness, and Experiencing the Divine. New World Library 2005 ISBN 1- 57731- 478- 6

Choquette, Sonia-*Trust Your Vibes The Secret Tools for Six Sensory Living.* Hay House Inc. 2004. ISBN 1-40190-232–4

Di Pego, Gerald *Phenomenon* Movie DVD 1996 Walt Disney Video Director Jon Turteltaub

Dyer, Dr. Wayne W. *The Power of Intention Learning to Co-create Your World Your Way.* Audio Cassettes Hay House Audio 2004 ISBN 1-4019-0315-0

Emoto,Masaru -- *The Hidden Messages in Water Beyond Words* Publishing 2004. Translated by David A. Thayne. www.beyondword.com ISBN 1-258270-114-8

Gelb, Michael J. *How to Think like Leonardo Da Vinci* Delacorte Press, 1998. ISBN 0-385-32381-6

Grabhorn, Lynn -- E*xcuse Me, Your Life Is Waiting The Astonishing Power of Feelings.* Hampton Roads Publishing Co. Inc. 2000, ISBN 1-57174-381–2

Hawkins, David R. M.D. Ph.D. *The Eye of the I* From Which Nothing Is Hidden Veritas Publishing ISBN 0-964-3261-9-1

Hawkins, David R, MD, Ph.D. *Power Versus Force* The Hidden Determinants of Human Behavior. Hay House Inc. 2002. ISBN 1- 56 170- 933- 6

Hicks, Jerry and Esther, *A New Beginning 1* Abraham-Hicks Publications 1988 ISBN 0 -9621219 -1-

Hicks, Jerry and Esther, *A New Beginning 2* Abraham-Hicks Publications 1991 ISBN 0 -- 9621219 - 1-6

Hicks, Esther and Jerry, *Ask and It Is Given, Learning to Manifest Your Desires* Hay House Inc. 2004. ISBN 1 - 4019 - 0459 - 9 www.Hayhouse.com

Hicks, Esther and Jerry, *The Amazing Power of Deliberate Intent Living the Art of Allowing* Hay House Inc. 2006. ISBN-13: 978-1-4019-0695-5 www.Hayhouse.com

Hill, Napoleon *Think and Grow Rich* audiotapes Audio Renaissance Tapes ISBN 0 -- 940687 -- 00 – 3

Holmes, Ernest, *the Science of Mind* A Philosophy, A Faith, A Way of Life. Jeremy P.Tarcher/Putnam, 1926. ISBN 0 -- 87477 -- 921 – 9

Hopkins, Tom, *How to Master the Art of Selling* Warner books, 1982. ISBN 0 -- 446 -- 386 36 -- 7

Kaufman, Barry Neil- *Happiness is a choice.* Fawcett Columbine, 1991 ISBN -- 0 -- 449 -- 90799 -- 6.

Langer Ellen J. *Mindfulness* Perseus books 1998. ISBN 0 -- 201 -- 09502 – 5

Langer, Ellen J. *On Becoming an Artist* Reinventing Yourself through Mindful Creativity, Ballantine books 2005. ISBN 0 -- 345 -- 45629 – 7

Laszlo, Ervin. *Science and the Akashic Field.* An Integral Theory of Everything. 2004 Inner Traditions ISBN 1-59477-042-5

Mails Thomas E. *Fools Crow* Power and Wisdom Council Oak books, 1991. ISBN 0 -- 933031 -- 35 – 1

Mails, Thomas E. *Fools Crow,* assisted by Dallas, Chief Eagle University of Nebraska press, 1979. ISBN 0 - 8032 -8174 - 9

McTaggart, Lynne, *The Field* The Quest for the secret force of the universe. Quill,2003. 2002 By HarperCollins. ISBN 0-06-019300-X

Milteer, Lee *Feel and Grow Rich* Hampton Roads, Publishing Co. Inc. 1993. ISBN 1 -- 878901 -- 88 – 5

Myss, Caroline Ph.D *Anatomy of the Spirit.* The Seven Stages of Power and Healing audiotapes Sounds True.

Nemeth, Ph.D., Maria *The Energy of Money*, a Spiritual Guide to Financial and Personal Fulfillment Ballantine Wellspring 1997 ISBN 0 -- 345 -- 43497 -- 8

Orloff, Judith M. D. *Positive Energy* 10 Extraordinary Prescriptions for Transforming Fatigue, Stress, and fear, Into Vibrance, Strength, and Love. Harmony books, 2004. ISBN 0 -- 609 -- 61010 – 4

Ostrander, Sheila, Schroeder, Lynn with Ostrander, Nancy *Super Learning* Delta/the Confucian press, 1979. ISBN 0 -- 385 -- 28952 -- 9

Ponder, Catherine -- *Open Your Minds to Prosperity,* Devorss 1983. ISBN 0 -- 87516 -- 531 – 1

Ramtha *The Magical Brain*: A Doorway to a Master's Reality. Video 1997, JZK, Inc.

Redfield, James *The Celestine Prophesy* An Adventure 1994 Warner Books ISBN 044651862X

Sudo, Philip Toshio-*Zen guitar* Fireside, Simon and Schuster, 1998. ISBN 0 -- 684 -- 83877 -- x.

Twist, Lynne -- *The Soul of Money* Transforming your Relationship with Money And Life. W.W. Norton & Co. Inc. 2003. ISBN 0 - 393 - 05097 –1

Twyman, James & Walsch, Neale Donald *Indigo* DVD Movie Emissary Productions 2005 Monterey Video

Walsch, Neale Donald, *Conversations with God,* An Uncommon Dialogue. Book 1. 1996 G.P. Putnam's Sons. ISBN 0-399-14278-9

Werner, Kenny -- *Effortless Mastery* Liberating the Master Musician with in. Jamie Aebersold, Jazz Inc. 1996 Http://www.Jajazz.com. ISBN 1 -- 56224 -- 003 – x

Wilde, Stewart *Life Was Never Meant to Be a Struggle, Hay House Inc. 1987 ISBN 1-56170-161- 0*

Williamson, Marianne A Return to Love 1996 Harper Collins ISBN0060927488

Audio Programs

Borysenko, Joan *The Power of the Mind to Heal* Renewing Body Mind and Spirit.

Choquette, Sonia *Your Psychic Pathway* Listening to the Guiding Wisdom of Your Soul.

Choquette, Sonia *Creating Your Heart's Desire* for Living the Life You Really Want.

Choquette, Sonia *True Balance* A Charka Guide for Renewing Your Body Mind and Spirit.

Canfield, Jack *How to Build High Self Esteem* Of Practical Process for Your Personal Growth.

Dyer, Dr. Wayne *The Universe within You* Your Secret Source of Strength.

Dyer, Dr. Wayne *The Awakened to Life* Beyond Success Achievement and Performance.

Dyer, Dr. Wayne *Transformation:* You'll See It When You Believe It.

Finley, Guy *The Secret of Letting Go* The Effortless Path To inner Success.

Jampolsky, Gerald G. M.D. & Cirincione, Diane V. *Attaining Inner Peace* Practical Applications of a Course in Miracles.

Cirincione, Diane V. & Jampolsky, Gerald G. M.D. *Creating Positive Relationships* Your Power to Turn Problems into Peace of Mind.

Lehrman, Fredric *Prosperity Consciousness* How to Tap Your Unlimited Wealth.

Levey, Joel and Michelle *The Focused Mind State* Maximizing Your Potential through the Power of Concentration.

Miller, Emmett M.D. *PowerVision* Life Mastery through Mental Imagery.

Peale, Norman Vincent *The Power of Positive Thinking.*

Peck, M. Scott, M.D. *The Road Less Traveled* A New Psychology of Love, Traditional Values and Spiritual Growth.

Robbins, Anthony *Unlimited Power* The New Science of Personal Achievement.

Wilde, Stuart *Infinite Self* 33 Steps to Reclaiming Your Inner Power.

Williamson, Marianne *Live* Lectures Based on a Course in Miracles.

Williamson, Marianne *On Practical Spirituality.*

All of the above audio programs are from the Nightingale Conant Corp.

Ed offers personal coaching and workshops on the law of attraction and self-esteem. For more information please visit our website:

www.BeYourBean.com

Dream your life. Live your dream.
Be your bean.™

www.BeYourBean.com

About the Author

Edward J. Langan is a musician, artist, and an award-winning photographer.

He has been on a spiritual quest for over 27 years studying everything from *A Course In Miracles* to quantum physics. He teaches workshops on Creating Consciously and Self-esteem. He lives in Massachusetts with his wife, Marjorie.

CPSIA information can be obtained
at www.ICGtesting.com
Printed in the USA
BVHW061525250322
632218BV00002B/154

9 780595 522163